Escape the Debt Trap

Let the Lord Lead You Out

Dr. Kregg Hood

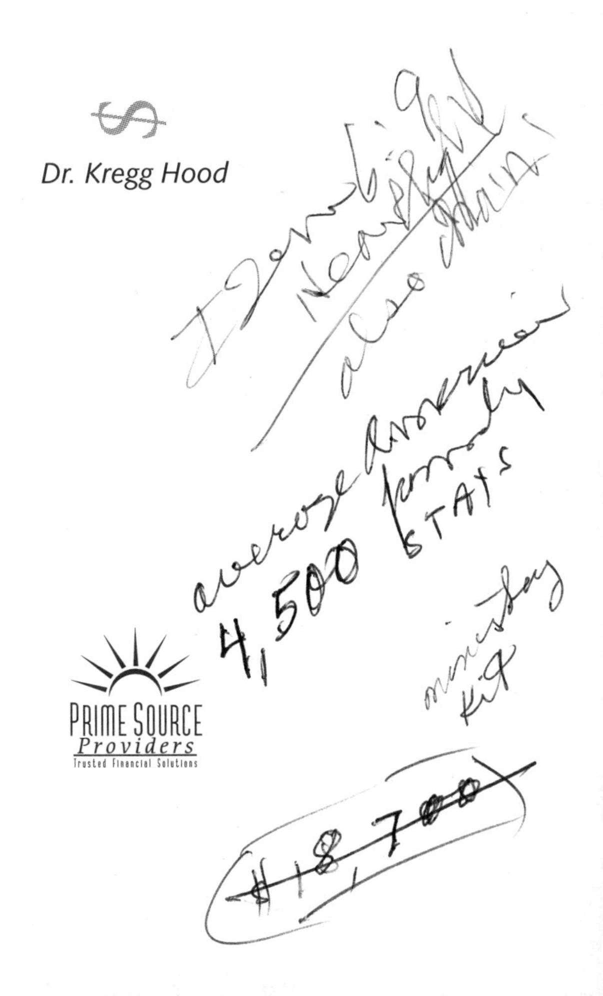

ESCAPE THE DEBT TRAP
Let the Lord Lead You Out

Published by Prime Source Providers
5750 Stratum
Fort Worth, TX 76137
800-364-5664

www.escapethedebttrap.com

Printed in the United States of America.

03 04 05 06 07 7 6 5 4 3 2 1

ISBN: 0-9729490-0-3

Contents

God is faithful; he will not let you be tempted beyond what you can bear. But when you are tempted, he will also provide a way out so that you can stand up under it.

—1 CORINTHIANS 10:13

chapter one

The Debt Trap

SHANIA TWAIN, one of the top country-pop singers of our time, has a song on her best-selling CD called "Ka-Ching." Her lyrics poke fun at the nonstop spending craze that's hit our culture. She sings that the desire for more never ends, so off everyone goes to the nearest shopping mall to spend what they don't have.

And I read an article on consumer debt in the newspaper where the first sentence blasted away, "Americans are on a borrowing binge that shows no sign of letting up." I shouldn't be amazed at news like this, but I have to admit that I shake my head in wonder. In spite of the concern that keeps hitting our economy, the amount of borrowing keeps growing because the appetite for spending is so hard to curb. For example, in 2001 banks that issued credit cards sent 5 billion pieces of mail to convince you and me to add just one new credit card to our wallets. Can you believe that families across America have more than 600 billion dollars in credit card debt? And worse still, that credit card debt alone averages more than eighty-three hundred dollars per household?

The 2002 statistics tell us that our nation is in real danger. This is how we handled the more than one trillion dollars in credit card purchases that year:

- An average of 14 percent of our income was consumed by credit card debt.
- Over 40 percent of us spent more than we earned, while our average savings rate was –2.2 percent. So as a nation, we spent more than we made!
- Over 50 percent of our households reported difficulty in making the minimum monthly payments on our credit cards.
- In June 2002 the Federal Reserve reported the total amount of all consumer debt was $1.685 trillion. Of that total, $660 billion was in credit card debt.

DEBT DAMAGES

Unless we allow God to strengthen our financial immune systems now, the damage to our finances, families, and faith will be life threatening. Let's examine how debt is damaging these significant areas of our lives.

Our Finances

Obviously, if 14 percent of the family income is spent on paying down credit card debt, there's less money to spend on current needs, save for the future, or invest in long-term goals. Another study reported that nearly half of all Americans (46 percent) had saved less than ten thousand dollars for retirement. Plus, since jobs and finances are tight for many in the current economy, the margin for error is very small. And if a payment is missed or late, huge fees hit the account and the interest rate could skyrocket. There are few or no reserve funds for emergencies. Plus, if a person pays only the minimum required on most credit cards, it could take decades to pay off an old debt. For example, if you make the minimum payment of a typical credit card balance of $4,800 (assuming an average interest rate of 17 percent, a common rate if your credit isn't really good), you can expect to pay on this amount for almost forty years! During that time, you'll pay close to $11,000 in interest payment alone. And this assumes you didn't charge anything new on the card.

Our Families

Current debt levels are adding stress to our families. In 2002, *USA Today* reported that over 40 percent of all consumers were close to running past their credit limits, that credit card late payments have now reached a five-year high, and that the amount of debt we're carrying on those cards is up 160 percent in the last ten years. Personal bankruptcies are at an all-time high, too. It's no wonder that financial stress is the number one reported cause of divorce. It's little wonder that, according to research from the Christian Stewardship Association, even though 91 percent said they made more money than ever, about 66 percent are more burdened financially than ever.

Our Faith

This leads me to two major concerns about our faith. First, debt keeps many Christians from giving to the Lord's work, which hinders the amount of ministry God calls us to do. I've run into this situation so frequently in ministry, so it's a major problem I'm here to address. Most Christians want to give but don't know how because they're carrying huge debt. They see giving as another debt obligation instead of a way to bless and be blessed.

And secondly, the most important spiritual effect of debt is what it does to our personal confidence in God. Out-of-control debt fuels desperation, depression, and fear. When afraid, we doubt. And when our doubt is stronger than our trust in a faithful God, we have a hard time grasping and relying on God's blessings. If Satan can use financial stress to steal our joy and damage our confidence in God's greatness and goodness, then we'll lose out on living full, healthy lives.

IMPULSE BUYING

Modern marketing methods capitalize on our impulsive buying nature. We see something that looks interesting, enjoyable, time saving, or just plain fun. If we are quick to use a credit card or an ATM machine, we can easily spend 20 percent more each month than we intended.

All it took was a few quick stops at the local convenience store or coffee shop on the way to work each week. Maybe it was a decision to buy something for the house that seemed pretty innocent because everyone in the family could enjoy it. But we didn't think through the number of payments we committed to before we signed on for another chunk of debt. Now include all those Christmas presents or the vacation that required borrowed money. While none of these purchasing decisions are inherently wrong, they may not be the wisest ways to use our money. Plus, if we are already in the Debt Trap, they're almost certainly not helping us get out. Getting out of the Debt Trap requires a different mind set altogether.

WHAT'S MESSING UP OUR THINKING?

When I ask people why we are struggling to live worry-free, God-honoring lives, here's what I usually hear:

- "Our young people just don't know how to manage their money."
- "People are selfish. They spend too much because they want too much."
- "Impatience is the problem. We live in the 'gotta-have-it-now!' world. Credit cards are too easy to use, so people don't say no."

While all three of these comments are accurate, I don't believe they get to the heart of the problem. If the problems were as simple as ignorance, selfishness, and impatience, then a good strong dose of discipline would help to straighten out our culture. The reality is that our problems are caused by something much more formidable. What's causing ignorance? What's causing selfishness? What's causing impatience? If we don't deal with the causes, it's a lot like going out to the backyard and mowing down the weeds rather than pulling them up by the roots. If all you do is mow the weeds, they'll just keep growing.

Easy access to consumer credit allows people to spend and max out the credit limit on a card, get another card, spend up to its limit, then get another one. The process continues until the person doing the spending can no longer afford to pay even the minimum required payments on the cards. A rising number who own homes are then refinancing their homes or taking out home equity loans, "cashing out" part of the equity and paying off the credit card bills. There's one big problem with this approach: If the spending patterns don't change they will be back in trouble shortly, and this time their home will be at risk. It's a classic case of treating symptoms, not causes. God wants to empower us to address the true causes.

THE POWER BEHIND TEMPTATION

Have you ever wondered what's behind your struggle with selfishness or impatience? Ephesians 6 and James 1 identify the real enemy: "Finally, be strong in the Lord and in his mighty power. Put on the full armor of God so that you can take your stand against the devil's schemes" (Ephesians 6:10–11). "When tempted, no one should say, "God is tempting me." For God cannot be tempted by evil, nor does he tempt anyone; but each one is tempted when, by his own evil desire, he is dragged away and enticed. Then, after desire has conceived, it gives birth to sin; and sin, when it is full-grown, gives birth to death" (James 1:13–15). Once we know what we're fighting, we'll change how we handle our problems with debt.

The reality is that we don't struggle with financial matters just because we're weak and ignorant, although that is often true, too. The fact is that the devil and his forces have schemes they use against us. They target the areas of our desire which are not governed by God, draw us away from wisdom, and then entice us to go deeper into error. If left unchecked, these schemes even open the door to sin. It's very important to understand that our being vulnerable to a scheme is not a sin. However, having a "spending weakness" is a danger sign that we're in the devil's crosshairs and that he plans to pull the trigger. If an assassin were stalking us, we would do everything possible to thwart his attempt on our life. Satan is a financial assassin who will use every weapon of financial pressure to lead us to panic and doubt God's goodness, mercy, and ability to rescue us from all our fears (Psalm 34:4).

Now that we know the source of our danger, the devil, we can learn how God wants to empower us by decreasing our vulnerabilities, avoiding the schemes, and escaping the Debt Trap. The first key is to realize our inability to whip these demons on our own. We need God. "Come near to God and he will come near to you. Wash your hands, you sinners, and purify your hearts, you double-minded" (James 4:8).

Debt is no different from any other burden or anxiety. Peter writes, "Cast all your anxiety on him because he cares for you" (1 Peter 5:7). So whether you're battling physical, spiritual, emotional, or financial problems, know that God cares and will lead you out of any trap. The devil would have you believe that finances are different, that God is only concerned about the spiritual stuff. That's an absolute lie. He cares about everything and he has the power to fulfill his purpose for us—abundant life. Solomon wrote, "It is not good to have zeal without knowledge, nor to be hasty and miss the way" (Proverbs 19:2). That's great news!

RECOGNIZING FOUR ENEMIES

Let's return to the weeds illustration. If ignorance, selfishness, and impatience are the weeds, what are the roots? Through Bible study, academic training, and practical ministry experience, I've noticed four main strategies used by the devil and his angels.[1] They are employed to produce every weakness or sin I know of. That is not an overstatement, either. Remember, Satan's primary goal is to destroy us and his primary tactic is deceit. If he can usurp God's leading authority by dispatching one or all of the following four enemies, you will be vulnerable in any arena in which he tries to attack you. Even though we'll see how he applies these strategies to financial matters, we will easily see that overpowering them will give us victory in many other areas of our lives, as well.

The devil uses feelings of inferiority, resentment, guilt, and fear to draw us away from God. They are more than mere emotions or psychological labels. They are calculating enemies that must be recognized and neutralized. Whenever the devil introduces any or all of these four enemies while we are consciously or subconsciously making a financial decision, the power of temptation escalates.

Satan uses the four enemies very cleverly, almost imperceptively so that he can slip in under our radar and do his damage. The first enemy is feelings of inferiority. Because they are "only feelings," they may not be recognized for what they really are. In our feeble attempts to deal with this enemy, we can run headlong into the next one—resentment. Resentment has many companions including bitterness and discontentment. Being weakened by the first two enemies, we are prime targets for the third—guilt. And if guilt doesn't bury us, the final enemy takes up residence—fear. Fear's companions of isolation and paralysis can keep us imprisoned in this vicious torture chamber of the four enemies for our entire lives until we decide to stop trying to resist them on our own. When we learn who the four enemies are and that God has a plan to empower our resistance, we can take control and escape. "Then you will know the truth, and the truth will set you free" (John 8:32).

1. *Feelings of inferiority*—I think this is the root enemy of them all, leading us in overspending. Something inside whispers,

You'll feel so much more worthwhile if you buy that house or that car. Many of us struggle with low self-esteem, rejection, or some form of inferiority. Signs of this enemy's presence include: being overly self-conscious, easily hurt or offended, deeply desiring attention, constantly comparing ourselves to others, and dominating or controlling others. Compensating for these uneasy or painful feelings by spending, consuming, and even flaunting a wealthy lifestyle has become some of the "quick fixes" of modern American society. And don't forget how fuzzy the definition of wealth is. What is wealthy to one person often seems poor to another. What might appear poor in one culture looks rich when you change the socioeconomic perspective. For example, two friends of mine were members of a church located in a very upscale neighborhood. Some of their wealthier friends noticed a really cute outfit their toddler son was wearing. When asked where they found it, the mom said she bought it at a discount store. The wealthier friend expressed shock, as if shopping at *that* store was beneath her. Now inferiority took the opportunity to manipulate both women—the one who apparently wouldn't be caught dead shopping at a discount store and my friend who was distressed that her friend thought less of her for shopping there. As crazy as it seems, this is exactly the way this enemy works. A couple of verses from Proverbs fit this setting: "One man pretends to be rich, yet has nothing; another pretends to be poor, yet has great wealth" (13:7). "A rich man may be wise in his own eyes, but a poor man who has discernment sees through him" (28:11). If you are buying in order to keep up with your peers, you are being dragged away by this enemy. One of two things will happen—either you'll spend yourself into the Debt Trap or you'll stop now and decide that your personal value has nothing to do with what *you buy.* It has everything to do with what Jesus paid to *buy you.* We all have infinite value regardless of our possessions, because the cost of Jesus' death on the cross was his priceless blood. "For you know the grace of our Lord Jesus Christ, that though he was rich, yet for your sakes he became poor, so that you through his poverty might become rich" (2 Corinthians 8:9). If Satan hasn't stirred the pot enough, or if he can find a foothold, he'll send resentment in to entrap you further.

2. *Resentment*—He and his evil ally bitterness like to work together. Whenever we find ourselves in a financial jam, they entice us to ask questions like, "Why did this happen to me?" When these enemies convince us to think we don't deserve this problem, our resentment breeds discontent. If allowed to continue unchecked, we might use spending as the only way to avoid these feelings. Another way this enemy works is when we resent a person. We may choose to spend our way into an appearance of superiority just to show off. We can even use money to hurt the other person. This spirit of retribution is based in the very source of this root of resentment: hate. That's a sobering thought!

But like an onion, resentment can be composed of a series of layers that have built up over time. To rid ourselves of resentment and its dangers to our spiritual and financial health, let's ask ourselves if we harbor any resentment toward our:

- Family's heritage—"I wish I hadn't grown up poor."
- Parents' financial situation—"My parents' financial mistakes have held me back."
- Lack of knowledge/intelligence—"If only I were as smart as other people, I'd have a better job."
- Physical appearance—"The boss gave the promotion to her only because she's more attractive."

- Skills and abilities—"I'm better suited for the job than he is. The boss ripped me off again."
- Job—"I'm stuck in a dead-end job."
- Spouse and children—"My family spends too much."

It is true that we didn't get to choose our parents or their income while we were growing up. No one asked us what gene pool we wanted to determine our skin, hair and eye color, or our body type. If we wanted the heredity and environment to play like a pro athlete, sing like an angel, think like Einstein, or make business deals to rival Warren Buffet, no one offered us the choice. But we can choose whether to honor or resent God for any or all of these things. Do you see where this is going? Resentment of any situation or person can ultimately indicate a hidden resentment of God. And that is a very scary thought. Honoring God with contentment will provide the antidote to eradicate this spiritual plague and will free us from the false cure of overspending. If you're struggling to find contentment, there is no more effective way to free your heart than to forgive. Stop holding your circumstances against others. Forgive and watch God work.

3. *Guilt*—After feelings of inferiority and resentment ensnare your heart and cloud your thinking, feelings of guilt slip in whenever Satan thinks you might be plotting an escape. He uses these feelings to remind you of the cost of your inadequacies and how much you owe others. Since you don't want others to pay the price for your failure, you are a prime target for this enemy's taunting. Feelings of guilt are closely tied to feelings of inferiority and serve as another source of overspending. Because we feel inferior, we feel unworthy of those we love. For example, if we're struggling to make ends meet, we

are tempted to keep using credit cards because we feel guilty that we cannot provide something that our loved ones really want. Parents, who are frequently away from their kids because of work or divorce, often overspend, thinking they can substitute nice things for time. Sometimes we believe we can buy the love or allegiance of our spouse or children if we haven't taken the time to invest ourselves in a real relationship with them. Maybe our selfishness, abusive behavior, or workaholism has robbed us of the time needed to build true relationships. All we are doing is taking a guilt trip in a car fueled by feelings of inferiority! See how these demonic forces work together to drive us further from God and his hope?

There is a distinct difference between feelings of guilt and the legal condition of guilt. The Bible refers to *guilty feelings* as "worldly sorrow" and to *conviction* as "godly sorrow" (2 Corinthians 7:10). Guilt leaves us feeling dirty and hopeless. Conviction makes us want to get clean and right with God and others. Guilty feelings lead to death while conviction leads to life. As a believer, all your sins were nailed to the cross with Christ. His sacrifice paid your guilt penalties. Knowing the difference, we can dramatically change the balance of power. Satan's power over us diminishes while God's power within us expands when we change and accept the freedom and confidence Jesus gives us.

4. *Fear*—By the time we've been in a life cycle of inferiority, resentment, and guilty feelings, the culminating result can be a life sentence, and fear is our jailer. We fear staying in the Debt Trap, but we're trapped by the fear of trying to escape. Fear can give way to panic, paralysis, and resignation. There is no escape—we are doomed. The reality is, with God you're never trapped because he is always in control.

God wants you to fear no one but him, since the fear of God is actually a source of protection. The Bible says, "The fear of the LORD is the beginning of wisdom, and knowledge of the Holy One is understanding" (Proverbs 9:10). Unless you confront the fear of failure, it will drive you to repeat the cycle of overspending.

ESCAPE THE TRAP

So how is your financial health? Are you suffering along with the national debt epidemic? If you're not, most likely someone you love is. Millions are suffering the ill effects of debt and see no cure or hope. But with God there is always hope. There is always a way of escape, because God's Word promises it (1 Corinthians 10:13). We don't have to remain trapped forever or die blaming ourselves with guilt for our mistakes.

We can escape resentment, guilt, fear, and the worst enemy of them all, feelings of inferiority. In order to find and use God's escape plan, we'll need to take God at his word in all financial matters, especially debt.

If you are managing your debt carefully and wisely, this book will give you ideas and advice to keep you out of trouble. I urge you to use your experience, and share what follows to help others who are imprisoned in the Debt Trap. On the other hand, if you're caught in the jaws of the Debt Trap now, there is real hope. With God's help you are going to get out. You can regain your financial health. Let's learn how.

ENDNOTE

1. *Prayer Can Change Your Life* by William Parker summarizes the way Satan schemes against us.

A man reaps what he sows. . . . Let us not become weary in doing good, for at the proper time we will reap a harvest if we do not give up.

—GALATIANS 6:7, 9

chapter two

The Universal Law

There is a fundamental law of the universe we need to believe and follow. It's the law of the harvest: You reap what you sow. In other words, what you plant determines what you get. The Bible puts it this way, "Do not be deceived: God cannot be mocked. A man reaps what he sows" (Galatians 6:7). This principle works whether we're talking about crops, friendships, spiritual growth, or finances. Since the financial crop many of us are reaping isn't so good, let's take a look at what and how we're sowing. If we're in the Debt Trap, the likelihood is great that we have at least one spending issue. Let's examine Galatians 6. The Bible gives us a very significant clue about what causes spending to get out of hand. Paul writes: "The one who sows to please his sinful nature, from that nature will reap destruction; the one who sows to please the Spirit, from the Spirit will reap eternal life. Let us not become weary in doing good, for at the proper time we will reap a harvest if we do not give up" (Galatians 6:8–9).

This passage tells us that when we sow to please our sinful nature the results are destruction. The phrase "sinful nature" is literally the word *flesh.* So when we sow primarily to please our flesh, we are making our physical wants, emotional desires, or psychological preferences the focus of our lives. Remember, this is the arena for the four enemies—feelings of inferiority, resentment, guilt, and fear. Since the result, mentioned in Galatians 6:8, is destruction or ruin the parallels to financial problems are clear. When we make decisions and take action with the satisfaction or appeasement of our fleshly desires as our primary goal, our outlook is bleak.

YOU REAP WHAT YOU THINK

We need to radically reorient our thinking and make new decisions before we can make our escape from the Debt Trap. The Bible has a word for the process of making new decisions: *repent.* Were there a few moans, or did someone mutter, "I don't want to read this next part?" Granted, *repent* is not a fun word to read, but let's think about what it means. Its basic definition is about more than quit-thinking-bad-and-start-thinking-good, although that is often the case. The basic definition is much more sweeping. Repent simply means to change your mind a complete 180 degrees. It involves the mental brainpower to reverse your course and the spiritual conviction to change behavior. The first step to a better harvest is sowing better seed. You absolutely will not get a better financial outcome without this first step.

The Bible is filled with truth for us about the power of our thinking. What would change if you allowed the following ideas and passages to guide your financial thinking, decisions, and practices?

Imagine the Lord being your "financial planner. "Search me, O God, and know my heart; test me and know my anxious thoughts" (Psalm 139:23). "You will keep in perfect peace him whose mind is steadfast, because he trusts in you" (Isaiah 26:3). "As the heavens are higher than the earth, so are my ways higher than your ways and my thoughts than your thoughts" (Isaiah 55:9).

Decide to think before you spend and don't believe every sales pitch you hear. "The wisdom of the prudent is to give thought to their ways, but the folly of fools is deception. . . . A simple man believes anything, but a prudent man gives thought to his steps" (Psalm 14:8, 15).

Let the Holy Spirit govern your mind in finances. The proof will be the presence of life and peace. "The mind of sinful man is death, but the mind controlled by the Spirit is life and peace" (Romans 8:6).

Think through the benefits or disadvantages of the proposed purchase, then decide. Are you being enticed by any or all of the four enemies to acquire things without a regard for the Lord's plan? Welcome to the oldest trick in the devil's book. "Do not love the world or anything in the world. If anyone loves the world, the love of the Father is not in him. For everything in the world—the cravings of sinful man, the lust of his eyes and the boasting of what he has and does—comes not from the Father but from the world. The world and its desires pass away, but the man who does the will of God lives forever" (1 John 2:15–17).

Let the Lord "renew" and "transform" your thinking. You will become a fantastic money manager! "Do not conform any longer to the pattern of this world, but be transformed by the renewing of your mind. Then you will be able to test and approve what God's will is—his good, pleasing and perfect will. For by the grace given me I say to every one of you: Do not think of yourself more highly than you ought, but rather think of yourself with sober judgment, in accordance with the measure of faith God has given you" (Romans 12:2–3).

Take every "purchasing thought" captive. How can any of the four enemies continue an attack when we boldly proclaim the following scripture during temptation? "The weapons we fight with are not the weapons of the world. On the contrary, they have divine power to demolish strongholds. We demolish arguments and every pretension that sets itself up against the knowledge of God, and we take captive every thought to make it obedient to Christ" (2 Corinthians 10:4–5).

When you're drawn to make an unwise purchase ask yourself: Is this purchase best for me and my loved ones? Is this the right time? Is it wise? Is there a better way to use this money? Stopping to both ask and answer these questions will revolutionize your spending.

Envision the Lord providing you with more wisdom, income, and perseverance. See him as the one who will rescue you from financial disappointment and ruin. "Yet this I call to mind and therefore I have hope: Because of the Lord's great love we are not consumed, for his compassions never fail. They are new every morning; great is your faithfulness. I say to myself, 'The LORD is my portion; therefore I will wait for him'" (Lamentations 3:21–26). Even though it may take time to experience full relief, remember that the same God who forgives all our sins and delivered Israel from physical bondage is the same God who saved Paul from death (2 Corinthians 1:8–11). If he can rescue us from these calamities, why are we hesitant to trust him through financial hardships?

Think ahead before you buy. Will you regret the purchase within a few months? How often have you bought something only to wish you had the money back? A friend of mine said, "I have the uneasy feeling that we're putting things out in the garage sale that still aren't paid off on our credit cards." If the four enemies haven't inflicted much damage to your finances, then the wisdom that comes with a few extra years of experience will probably help you to put some childish spending patterns behind you. "When I was a child, I talked like a child, I thought like a child, I reasoned like a child. When I became a man, I put childish ways behind me" (1 Corinthians 13:11). However, if you are in trouble and need to grow up fast, following this godly advice can shorten your learning curve! Enjoy what you have now.

Think about the positive side of being out of debt. "Finally, brothers, whatever is true, whatever is noble, whatever is right, whatever is pure, whatever is lovely, whatever is admirable—if anything is excellent or praiseworthy—think about such things" (Philippians 4:8). I could keep going, but this final passage sums up the purpose of reading and applying these passages specifically to finances. This is a financial picture I like to envision:

- "Whatever is true"—believing in God's principles for money management.
- "Whatever is noble"—giving money to change lives for God, rather than going down the drain on interest payments.
- "Whatever is right"—saving and spending as a wise steward of the resources God has given me.
- "Whatever is pure"—knowing that I'm not buying things that displease or break God's heart.
- "Whatever is lovely"—preventing the stress of heavy payments or harassing bill collectors calling all the time.
- "Whatever is admirable"—building up resources for future use in giving, retirement, or other God-honoring activities.

Wouldn't a financial picture like this be excellent and praiseworthy? Certainly! Think about it happening. Believe

God will change your fortunes, literally. You will begin to reap good results as you decide to change your thinking.

PREVENT CROP FAILURE

Want to ensure your financial crop and experience freedom from the Debt Trap? Use God's ways to prevent crop failure. Remember, even though we'll apply these tactics to finances, you can use them whenever the devil moves in to steal, kill, or destroy:

1. Repent. Now is the time to decide to reject the world's philosophies about money, wealth, spending, and debt. Determine to align your heart with God's heart on *every* subject. If there are any topics where you've allowed the devil to draw you away and entice you, take your stand. For example, if you know you've used your money foolishly, admit it, confess it, and decide to start fresh. God will let you. If you've failed to take the time to learn wise, biblical principles of money management, repent and get started on a new path. Don't wait another day. If fear has immobilized you regarding some financial issue, recognize that this fear is the enemy fear, not the fear of God. It's from the Evil One. That's why the most frequent command from Jesus was "fear not."

If you're battling guilt and allowing it to motivate spending urges, determine to replace guilt with a confidence that God will meet all your needs and the needs of your loved ones (Philippians 4:19). I love what the psalmist said, "My flesh and my heart may fail, but God is the strength of my heart and my portion forever" (Psalm 73:26). God is there for us, and he is truly enough. If feelings of inferiority plague you and incite your heart, claim the victory of Jesus over all aspects of your life. And if resentment or bitterness are fueling unwise spending, remember how God's love is the strongest force in the universe. Get God's heart and everything else will fall into place.

2. Soak up the Scriptures. Read the Bible more consistently and watch for passages that give you insight and strength. Read this passage that battles all four enemies, "His divine power has given us everything we need for life and godliness through our knowledge of him who called us by his own glory and goodness. Through these he has given us his very great and precious promises, so that through them you may participate in the divine nature and escape the corruption in the world caused by evil desires" (2 Peter 1:3–4). Other passages like Proverbs 22:1–2 keep me thinking straight: "A good name is more desirable than great riches; to be esteemed is better than silver or gold. Rich and poor have this in common: The Lord is the Maker of them all."

One of the more interesting ways to study the Bible is to use a computer concordance to look up all passages that include words like *wealth, riches,* or *money.* It's a massive amount of wisdom about what to do with money. God's Word teaches us how to make money, spend money, and give money. The more we know of God's Word or any topic, the better prepared we'll be when we come up against one of the devil's schemes.

Jesus used this approach when he was tempted, too. In Matthew 4:1–11 the devil hit Jesus with an assault that included extreme hunger, physical safety, and personal value. Each attack parallels the same financial issues we have today. In each case, Jesus responded by quoting a passage from the Scriptures to Satan. This one action has totally convinced me that there is no substitute for acquiring an intimate knowledge of the Word of God. Jesus knew the Scriptures so well that when attacked by the devil, he whipped out a response that literally ended each attack. That is amazing! Jesus' recall was quick, relevant, and precise. Jesus did this to show us how to win, too.

- Imagine proactively attacking the financial strongholds in your life the way Jesus did.
- When afraid, remember Hebrews 13:5–6, "Keep your lives free from the love of money and be content with what you have, because God has said, 'Never will I leave you; never will I forsake you.' So we say with confidence, 'The Lord is my helper; I will not be afraid. What can man do to me?'"
- When feeling guilty about past financial mistakes, read the parable of the prodigal son (Luke 15:11–32). This is such an appropriate story. The son abandons his father to pursue a reckless spending spree. Unknown to him, his father longingly scans the horizon anticipating his eventual return. As you read the story, visualize yourself as the spending prodigal and God as your loving Father. He is scanning the horizon anticipating your return and the opportunity to welcome you home. Let the joy of that reunion sink in and take root in your thinking: He is waiting to take you back.
- When feeling inferior to others because you lack financial status, remember that God sees great value in humble circumstances (James 1:9–11) and that, in reality, a simpler lifestyle has its advantages as well. "Better a little with the fear of the LORD than great wealth with turmoil" (Proverbs 15:16).
- When tempted to resent someone and prove your strength over them, remember that it is always God's place to bring justice (Romans 12:17–21). Our place is with the power of

generosity. "Command those who are rich in this present world not to be arrogant nor to put their hope in wealth, which is so uncertain, but to put their hope in God, who richly provides us with everything for our enjoyment. Command them to do good, to be rich in good deeds, and to be generous and willing to share. In this way they will lay up treasure for themselves as a firm foundation for the coming age, so that they may take hold of the life that is truly life" (1 Timothy 6:17-19). God's Word is a powerful weapon in your fight against the devil (Hebrews 4:12–13). Nothing in all creation is hidden from God's sight.

3. Renew your spirit. The challenge to reap a good crop and change your financial harvest is also a call to prayer. In the Lord's Prayer, Jesus gave us permission, even a command, to pray for our daily bread (Matthew 6:11). Philippians 4:6–7 tells us, "Do not be anxious about anything, but in everything, by prayer and petition, with thanksgiving, present your requests to God. And the peace of God, which transcends all understanding, will guard your hearts and your minds in Christ Jesus." This means our financial anxieties really belong at Jesus' feet.

Try this: Specifically lay your financial issues and burdens by name at the feet of the cross. Repent by renouncing any fears, issues of guilt, feelings of inferiority, or reasons for resentment. Every time you do this, you defeat the four enemies! You will reap an immediate harvest of peace when you give these circumstances, along with their causes, to God. Let him show you the way. Let him shut bad doors and open good ones (Deuteronomy 8:18; Proverbs 10:22). Let him lead you to a better job or encourage you to be a more positive and productive worker while you wait for a new opportunity (1 Corinthians 7:21).

Every battle needs the Lord's hand. Pray and give him time to work. Renewing your spirit actually lifts your spirits, too. Another passage that blesses me deeply is this: "Rejoice in the Lord always. I will say it again: Rejoice! Let your gentleness be evident to all. The Lord is near" (Philippians 4:4–5). This message opens the door of our hearts to worship God, even when we don't feel like it. When I was battling a major financial issue at work, my wife gave me a worship CD for my birthday by Christian artist Michael W. Smith. The recording, entitled very simply *Worship* begins with the song "Forever." As I drove to the office I listened to this declaration:

Forever God is faithful
Forever God is strong
Forever God is with us
Forever.[1]

I can't describe the peace and faith that rose up inside me. I replayed the song three or four times that morning and prayed a prayer of thanksgiving for the certainty that he would be with me. I felt very grateful for many blessings that we often take for granted—health, friendships, food, and so on. It was a special "God encounter" I'll never forget. Now, that's a birthday present!

At other difficult times in my life, I've drawn great strength and encouragement from the hymn "Be Still My Soul." The first verse says:

Be still my soul, the Lord is on thy side.
Bear patiently the cross of grief or pain.
Leave to thy God to order and provide;

In every change, He faithful will remain.
Be still, my soul: thy best, thy heavenly Friend
Through thorny ways leads to a joyful end.

And perhaps my all-time favorite, no matter what the trial is, the powerful classic "Great Is Thy Faithfulness." The chorus *always* brings tears to my eyes. It comes directly from Scripture in Lamentations 3:22.

Great is thy faithfulness
Great is thy faithfulness
Morning by morning, new mercies I see.
All I have needed thy hand hath provided;
Great is thy faithfulness, Lord unto me.[2]

When I battle any problem, including financial fears and crises, I find that God renews my spirit through prayer, praise, and worship. When the devil attacks you, make him miserable, too. Nothing frustrates the plans of the Enemy like sincere, determined worship. Words of worship must sound to Satan like fingernails scratching on a chalkboard. Praise expresses your love, confession cleanses your heart and soul, and thanksgiving proclaims your confidence in God to sustain you, no matter what.

4. Reach out to others. Whenever we are being deceived by the devil, we are susceptible to another lie—that we're all alone. We are afraid that we're the only one who doesn't have our act together, and fear won't let us admit it to others. In reality, a significant percentage of people we know are silently stuck in the Debt Trap. We've already seen the statistics. If the *average* American household now has more than eighty-three hundred dollars in credit card debt, we know that we have lots of company. An executive director of a nonprofit consumer credit counseling organization told me he believes between 10 and 15 percent of all households in America should probably consider seeking professional help for formulating a debt management plan to correct their problems. He also told me that, ideally, there is no organization in the country better suited to provide encouragement in these matters than the church. Imagine the good that will be done when we create a safe, secure place for Christians to give and receive wise, biblical advice in the area of finances! It will dramatically impact our society.

If you're in the Debt Trap, reach out to someone who can help you. Allow yourself to experience healthy accountability. As Ecclesiastes 4:9–10 says, "Two are better than one, because they have a good return for their work: If one falls down, his friend can help him up. But pity the man who falls and has no one to help him up!" A couple of other passages underscore the value of advisers: "Plans fail for lack of counsel, but with many advisers they succeed. . . . Make plans by seeking advice; if you wage war, obtain guidance" (Proverbs 15:22; 20:18).

Others help us see what we cannot see for ourselves. Plus, there is a healthy pressure in having someone examine our decisions and encourage us to do what God will bless. Make sure that anyone you reach out to is spiritual, gentle, and humble (Galatians 6:1). Find someone you trust and let them help. You can do this one-on-one or by joining a financial ministry small group at church. If your congregation doesn't have a program like this, talk to your leadership about starting one. We offer resources you can tap into at the end of the last chapter. Volunteer to help because the process of learning how to help others will benefit you, as well. This is part of the promise of

Proverbs 11:25, "A generous man will prosper; he who refreshes others will himself be refreshed."

When you reach out to others, both in seeking and offering help, you will break free from feelings of isolation. Satan will have a harder time messing up your thinking when he no longer has a captive audience.

5. Draw close to Jesus. We all need to realize that he is our true source of strength, and he deserves more than mere lip service. Drawing close isn't for his benefit—it's for ours! There is enormous strength to overcome the Evil One when our hearts and lives are submitted to the Lord. One of the best Bible stories illustrating this point is in Acts 19:13–20:

> Some Jews who went around driving out evil spirits tried to invoke the name of the Lord Jesus over those who were demon-possessed. They would say, "In the name of Jesus, whom Paul preaches, I command you to come out." Seven sons of Sceva, a Jewish chief priest, were doing this. One day the evil spirit answered them, "Jesus I know, and I know about Paul, but who are you?" Then the man who had the evil spirit jumped on them and overpowered them all. He gave them such a beating that they ran out of the house naked and bleeding. When this became known to the Jews and Greeks living in Ephesus, they were all seized with fear, and the name of the Lord Jesus was held in high honor. Many of those who believed now came and openly confessed their evil deeds. A number who had practiced sorcery brought their scrolls together and burned them publicly. When they calculated the value of the scrolls, the total came to fifty thousand drachmas. In this way the word of the Lord spread widely and grew in power.

This story tells me that if we try to pull the weeds of inferiority, resentment, guilt, and fear with any strength other than that which comes through a relationship with Jesus, we are setting ourselves up for miserable failure. The enemies who entice us to spend foolishly do not give up easily.

If we have repeatedly tried and failed to get our financial messes under control, could it be that we haven't made Jesus our financial manager? Fellowship with Jesus, not just financial know-how or money sense will carry us to freedom. The apostle John writes, "If we claim to have fellowship with him yet walk in the darkness, we lie and do not live by the truth. But if we walk in the light, as he is in the light, we have fellowship with one another, and the blood of Jesus, his Son, purifies us from all sin" (1 John 1:6–7). See that? The purifying power is in fellowship with Jesus. It's found in seeing him as a friend and relying on him as a leader for our lives. The same biblical author writes this a little further in his letter: "And this is the testimony: God has given us eternal life, and this life is in his Son. He who has the Son has life; he who does not have the Son of God does not have life" (1 John 5:11–12). I want *life* in all my dealings. I want life in my walk with the Lord, in my family relationships, with the people I work with, in the situations where I make an income. I want life to come into my emotional health and my views about the future. And, of course, I want life in my finances. The Debt Trap creates death, but the signature of God's way is righteousness, peace, and joy (Romans 14:17).

The universal law is for real—what we sow truly determines what we reap. And what we reap begins with how we think. Once we use God's seed and his approach to planting, we'll begin to harvest a new future.

ENDNOTES

1. Taken from "Forever" by Chris Tomlin © Six Steps Music/ Worship Together Songs. All rights reserved. Used by permission.

2. Taken from "Great Is Thy Faithfulness" by Thomas O. Chisholm © 1923. Renewal 1951 Hope Publishing Co., Carol Stream, IL 60188. All rights reserved. Used by permission.

Seek first his kingdom and
his righteousness, and all these
things will be given to you as well.

—MATTHEW 6:33

chapter three

The Guarantee

PEOPLE from the West African Maninka tribe are known to say this proverb: "The man who tries to walk two roads will split his pants." No commentary on Matthew 6:33 could be more correct!

One day as Jesus spoke to a large crowd, he dealt with the same basic economic issues that concern us today: "So do not worry, saying, 'What shall we eat?' or 'What shall we drink?' or 'What shall we wear?' For the pagans run after all these things, and your heavenly Father knows that you need them. But seek first his kingdom and his righteousness, and all these things will be given to you as well" (Matthew 6:31–33). What a guarantee!

Daily concerns haven't changed much in two thousand years have they? We've been asking those same questions since before the time of Christ: What will we eat? What will we wear? In short, how do we pay the bills, live our lives, and get by? These issues have had a strangle hold on everyday folks across the millennia. So the answer for them fits us, too: Seek first the kingdom of God.

Every time I read verse 33 I am amazed that God puts his integrity on the line with us. He actually defines himself as our provider and leader! He will provide for us, he will lead us, he will bring good things to our lives. These things, the necessities of life, *will be* given; God guarantees it. And we put all this in motion by placing God's kingdom at the top of our priority list. By aggressively placing this priority above all others—above our wants, our desires, our perceptions of need, our relationships and more—we allow God to provide for us and lead us. We can't be passive about it. I believe this directive tells us to make a very definite and deliberate choice to seek the kingdom of God or else the devil will trick us into focusing on our worries, wants, and weaknesses. Seeking God this way results in true liberation! Now all these things will be *given to us.* Imagine that? Following God will lead us to have the resources to buy our food, clothing, and other items necessary for life. Not only will "these things" be provided, but a life that's worth living. I've never seen the world's system offer a guarantee like that, have you?

FOLLOWING THE WRONG SYSTEM

We already know we're in a financial mess and one of the ways we got there was the same way those first century folks did—by following the lead of the world's economic system instead of the lead of God. For decades our government has relied on deficit spending. Our businesses require massive amount of credit to expand and operate, and some require credit to simply survive. It is no surprise then, that individuals have both easy access to credit, which helps them spend, and high debts, the result of using that credit to spend.

The majority of Americans have grown up during times of great economic expansion. We've come to believe that the American dream is our birthright. But has this expansion produced fewer problems or stronger families? Poverty, racial distress, job insecurity, and emotional stress are steadily increasing. The issues of credit and debt are very emotional; your experience will greatly affect your conclusions. If you've had good experiences with credit, you'll see it as a positive tool for financing your life and business. But if debt has hurt you or you've been taught that all debt is either unwise or sinful, you'll do your best to get out of it or avoid it. My approach strikes a balance between these two conclusions.

SPIRITUAL PRINCIPLE VS. FINANCIAL PRACTICE

At what point do our principles and practices coincide instead of collide? How do we blend the spiritual principle of seeking God first with both daily and long-term financial practices? If we truly desire to seek God first, we need to acquire his unique perspective. The best place to acquire that perspective is his Word. Let God's Word provide the boundaries for your personal conclusions about borrowing, debt, credit, and spending. If you are already making financial decisions from God's perspective, you will continue to stand on solid ground. If your current ground is more like quicksand, following these perspectives should help you gain better footing as you get ready to make your escape from the Debt Trap.

Perspective 1: Debt and Borrowing

The Bible actually says a lot about debt and borrowing. First, it's clear that it would be better not to have to borrow. Proverbs 22:7 says, "The rich rule over the poor, and the borrower is servant to the lender." Several ideas are especially significant. For example, the word *rule* indicates the control that financial matters exert. So decisions and circumstances which cause your options to be reduced or take control out of your hands and the Lord's and place them in the hands of another are not optional. Another word in this passage that grips me is the word *servant.* This is the same word that is often translated "slave" in the Bible. The Israelites in Egypt were servants of Pharaoh, living under his rule, controlled by his desires. Got the picture? As long as you owe someone a debt, in that area they are the ruler and you are the slave. In fact, in this area, God made it clear that his desire was for Israel to do the lending and not the borrowing. "For the Lord your God will bless you as he has promised, and you will lend to many nations but will borrow from none. You will rule over many nations but none will rule over you. . . . The Lord will open the heavens, the storehouse of his bounty, to send rain on your land in season and to bless all the work of your hands. You will lend to many nations but will borrow from none" (Deuteronomy 15:6; 28:12).

At the same time, if one of God's people loaned money to another Israelite, this was allowable. However, no interest was to be charged. It was, in essence, a no-interest loan. "If you lend money to one of my people among you who is needy, do not be like a moneylender; charge him no interest" (Exodus 22:25). "If there is a poor man among your brothers in any of the towns of the land that the Lord your God is giving you, do not be hardhearted or tightfisted toward your poor brother. Rather be openhanded and freely lend him whatever he needs" (Deuteronomy 15:7–8). God's heart was with the poor and needy, and it's obvious from Scripture that rather than create a money-hungry culture, the Lord wanted to cultivate a "money-service" culture where financial resources are seen as a tool for good, not selfish gain or greed: "Good will come to him who is generous and lends freely, who conducts his affairs with justice" (Psalm 112:5). "He who is kind to the poor lends to the LORD, and he will reward him for what he has done" (Proverbs 19:17).

Note the words of Jesus himself:

> Give to the one who asks you, and do not turn away from the one who wants to borrow from you. (Matthew 5:42)

> And if you lend to those from whom you expect repayment, what credit is that to you? Even "sinners" lend to "sinners," expecting to be repaid in full. But love your enemies, do good to them, and lend to them without expecting to get anything back. Then your reward will be great, and you will be sons of the Most High, because he is kind to the ungrateful and wicked. Be merciful, just as your Father is merciful. (Luke 6:34–36)

> Then he said to them, "Suppose one of you has a friend, and he goes to him at midnight and says, 'Friend, lend me three loaves of bread, because a friend of mine on a journey has come to me, and I have nothing to set before him.' Then the one inside answers, 'Don't bother me. The door is already locked, and my children are with me in bed. I can't get up and give you anything.' I tell you, though he will not get up and give him the bread because he is his friend, yet because of the man's boldness he will get up and give him as much as he needs. So I say to you: Ask and it will be given to you; seek and you will find; knock and the door will be opened to you. For everyone who asks receives; he who seeks finds; and to him who knocks, the door will be opened. Which of you fathers, if your son asks for a fish,

> will give him a snake instead? Or if he asks for an egg, will give him a scorpion? If you then, though you are evil, know how to give good gifts to your children, how much more will your Father in heaven give the Holy Spirit to those who ask him!" (Luke 11:5–13)

Paul quoted Jesus, too:

> In everything I did, I showed you that by this kind of hard work we must help the weak, remembering the words the Lord Jesus himself said: "It is more blessed to give than to receive." (Acts 20:35)

> He who has been stealing must steal no longer, but must work, doing something useful with his own hands, that he may have something to share with those in need. Do not let any unwholesome talk come out of your mouths, but only what is helpful for building others up according to their needs, that it may benefit those who listen. (Ephesians 4:28–29)

Take note of these passages in which Elisha, Nehemiah, and Jesus instructed individuals concerning borrowing and lending:

> She went and told the man of God, and he said, "Go, sell the oil and pay your debts. You and your sons can live on what is left." (2 Kings 4:7)

> What you are doing is not right. Shouldn't you walk in the fear of our God to avoid the reproach of our Gentile enemies? I and my brothers and my men are also lending the

> people money and grain. But let the exacting of usury stop! Give back to them immediately their fields, vineyards, olive groves and houses, and also the usury you are charging them—the hundredth part of the money, grain, new wine and oil. (Nehemiah 5:9–11)

> Give to the one who asks you, and do not turn away from the one who wants to borrow from you. (Matthew 5:42)

Those verses indicate that loaning and borrowing were allowed along with this principle:

> The wicked borrow and do not repay, but the righteous give generously. (Psalm 37:21)

Integrity is the core issue:

> I know, my God, that you test the heart and are pleased with integrity. All these things have I given willingly and with honest intent. And now I have seen with joy how willingly your people who are here have given to you. (1 Chronicles 29:17)

All of these verses and many more should soften our hearts toward the ultimate objective—possessing God's heart about the use of money in general before we can ever hope to manage credit and debt. Perhaps you've heard Christian leaders debate whether debt is scriptural or unscriptural. Regardless of anyone's position, we must first pin down the issue of seeking God first. We can easily become covetous in overspending, the obvious point, but we can also become covetous in extreme frugality if our focus gives us a harsh attitude on saving money, reducing spending, and criticizing those who disagree. Let's all take a deep breath and seek the Lord.

The Word of God leads us to conclude these three points about borrowing:

1. It's best not to put yourself in the position of the borrower whenever possible.
2. Borrowing was allowed and interest was not automatically outlawed.
3. If you must borrow, pay it back. Keep your word about repayment.

The bottom line with credit debt in the Bible is that the lender should not take advantage of the person in financial distress and the borrower should keep his word and pay back the loan.

Romans 13:8 is frequently quoted to outlaw all borrowing by a believer. The King James Version is especially strict here. It reads, "Owe no man any thing, but to love one another: for he that loveth another hath fulfilled the law." I believe that the New International Version renders a more accurate translation here. It reads: "Let no debt remain outstanding, except the continuing debt to love one another, for he who loves his fellowman has fulfilled the law." Actually, the phrase "owe no man anything" is better translated "Do not continue to owe anything to anyone." Personally, I take that to mean don't get behind on your payments, which is another way of keeping your word. If I borrow money from a bank to buy my house, I agree to pay them a set amount of dollars by a certain date each month until the house is paid for. I'm being honest when I pay them back according to our agreed upon schedule. I made a promise I should keep. That attitude pleases God and gives Christians a positive testimony. And the principle is true whether we're talking about a house, a car, or credit card payment. It is a related but separate decision from why I would make the spending decision in the first place.

Now let's look more closely at the context of the verse. The setting actually has nothing to do with our banking and borrowing practices. It really says the issue above all is love. The one thing we're always to pay and repay is love. We never get out of debt in the interpersonal relations arena because of what Jesus did at the cross. It's almost a restatement of the Golden Rule: "Do to others what you would have them do to you" (Matthew 7:12). So in reality, this passage targets how we treat others and really has no direct bearing on the question of whether a Christian can go into debt. Make up your own mind to be honest in all your financial matters (honest with others, yourself, and with God, the one you want to hear say, "Well done good and faithful servant."

Perspective 2: Spending

Even though there is no clean-cut prohibition in Scripture against debt, it's obvious that many people are being demolished by problems related to it. Therefore, God must have answers for us. In 2 Peter 1:3 he says, "His divine power has given us everything we need for life and godliness through our knowledge of him who called us by his own glory and goodness." Previously we looked at the tactics of the four enemies who entice us to overspend or to spend unwisely. Gaining a wisdom mentality will prepare you to ask questions that will thwart these tactics.

Can I afford it? This is a great wisdom question. In chapter 4 we'll address the in-depth specifics of this question. But for now, let's hit the high points, based on our desire for God's wisdom. One of the issues related to affording a purchase is not can I but should I? To illustrate, let's say you have a good, steady income. You work hard and your income would allow you to qualify for and actually purchase a larger home or a nicer car or a special vacation. Rather than simply assume that because you *can* purchase a particular item, why not pray and ask the Lord for his mind and heart on the matter? Remember as you pray that God is a good God (1 Chronicles 16:34) and that he "richly provides us with everything for our enjoyment" (1 Timothy 6:17). So don't assume God is trying to steal your joy or take away fun. His concern is for the bigger questions of life—do you trust his guarantee? Will he protect you from harm and equip you to do good? As you pray for wisdom, ask him:

- Will this purchase place a strain on my budget?
- How will this purchase affect my long-term financial goals (retirement, education, debt repayment, etc.)?
- If my income dropped suddenly and I needed to sell the item, would I be able to pay off the debt?
- Will this purchase make it hard for me to give to the Lord's work?
- What effects will this purchase have on my time with family and friends?
- How will this purchase affect my ability to minister to others?

If you can honestly answer all these questions and any others that come to your mind, in a positive way you may well be on safe footing in the proposed purchase. Stay alert to possible "blind sides" based on your desires or personality, especially where large sums of money are involved. One of my best friends is an astute, successful, and seasoned business leader who often reminds me, "You know what you know, but you don't know what you don't know." The best deals in the world can turn sour pretty fast. I have personal experience with both the good and the bad.

As you plan to purchase a home, a car, or any other item that requires years to pay off, plan on buying *less* than the maximum level the decision makers in the lending company say you can afford. We all know of those who purchased more house or car than they could comfortably pay for. Then when their income dropped, or they tried to free up more funds for giving, for a college education, or even for paying off credit card debt, they realized that they were caught in the Debt Trap.

Perspective 3: Credit

When making wisdom decisions about using credit, think about James 4:13–15. It's a great passage for keeping us on target: "Now listen, you who say, 'Today or tomorrow we will go to this or that city, spend a year there, carry on business and make money.' Why, you do not even know what will happen tomorrow. What is your life? You are a mist that appears for a little while and then vanishes. Instead, you ought to say, 'If it is the Lord's will, we will live and do this or that.'" The context of this passage has to do with business. We don't know what tomorrow will be like in any arena (health, relationship, or finances).

While meeting with the president of a successful company in the consumer credit industry, we talked about the problems of debt and credit. He said credit is like a lever—a tool people need to learn to use carefully in their personal financial issues. Credit, he pointed out, has allowed people to purchase valuable assets and pay for them over time, which is good. At the same time, he was concerned about the runaway levels of consumer debt in our society and made a strong case for teaching people, especially students and young adults, how to use credit wisely.

This leads me to draw an important distinction between credit and debt. Credit, in its basic form, is a tool we use to make a purchase. Debt is the result of making that purchase. If credit is used to purchase an asset that has excellent potential to increase in value, then the purchase decision may be a good one. For example, few people have the cash just lying around to buy a house, an education, or a business. So if the asset is truly worth owning and the borrower can afford to make the necessary payments to repay the lender, then using credit may be the wisest course of action. Biblically, I want to always remind myself that since God owns everything (1 Chronicles 29:11, 14), I should do my best to prayerfully consider whether or not God wants me to "own" this asset under his sovereign control.

Remember to keep the focus on God and his will. He has the power to provide his favor in all areas of our life, including our finances. God is the one who gives us the ability to make wealth (Deuteronomy 8:17). Before using credit to get into debt, get the Lord's perspective.

What about credit cards? This is a very controversial topic, especially among Christians who teach, preach, and counsel on this issue. The positives on the use of credit cards are obvious:

- Convenience—They are easy to carry around and accepted in most stores.

- Security—There is no need to carry large amounts of cash since the card is accepted for most purchases. You are also protected against most fraudulent usages. Plus, many credit cards have extended services available which give purchase protection from bogus or shady merchants, extra warranty coverage, and even protection against loss, theft, or damage.
- Record keeping—Transaction information can be downloaded into computer programs for money management, allowing for an easy spending analysis. Some people even carry multiple cards and dedicate one for personal use and one for business use.
- Extra benefits—Some cards pay the cardholder "points" that can be redeemed for airline travel, hotel stays, and merchandise.
- Low or no-interest balance transfers—If a person's credit is good, credit cards can be used to pay off existing higher interest debt and transfer that debt to a lower interest rate alternative.

At the same time, each of these benefits has a dark side that can trip you up:

- Convenience is one of the major reasons why we spend more than we realize. Research indicates that extensive credit card purchasing leads to 112 percent greater spending than a cash only approach.
- Security has a drawback, since even though you're protected against fraudulent usage, the fact that you participate in the world of electronic finance means the probability increases that you could be the victim of

"identity theft." In this rapidly growing scenario, someone finds out your personal information that uniquely identifies you and then begins opening up accounts as if they were you! While you can ultimately get the problems all sorted out if this happens, the time, effort, and energy you invest fighting could be significant. This has already happened to me, I might add.

- The record keeping drawback is marginal. The main thing to remember is to actually use the benefit to help you become more effective and efficient in your spending practices.
- Extra benefits are only a benefit if they're worth the extra cost of having them. Airline-related cards almost always have a yearly membership fee added on. Plus, be careful about making an unnecessary purchase just to get your airline miles. If you do, you wind up back in the first category of drawbacks that come from convenience.
- Low or no-interest deals are also potential headaches, if not outright nightmares. Read the fine print carefully. Do you have to pay a balance-transfer fee? How long will the lower interest rate last? What happens if you're late on even one payment? Most of these offers give the bank the right to jack up the interest rate immediately to a horrible rate. Also, don't forget that many people are using these come-ons to get into deeper debt. Rather than curb their urge to overspend, they simply get a new card with a fresh credit line and a low or no-interest rate, transfer their old balances, then keep on spending. They tend to pay only the minimum required payments, too. So over the next few months their total indebtedness goes higher and higher. Eventually, they hit the point of no return. Once

their credit is maxed out and their debt load becomes unmanageable, they are deeply caught in the Debt Trap because of these "deals."

RULES FOR USING CREDIT CARDS

When it comes to credit card use, I can't say, "Just say no." The benefits are worth using them, especially if you're a business traveler. However, if you're going to use credit cards, remember these important two rules:

1. Pay off the entire balance every month. The first month you can't pay the card off, red lights should flash and the warning buzzer should sound. Remember, it's a credit card not a debt card.
2. Keep your purchases under budget. Credit cards make it so incredibly easy to overspend. Guard this decision carefully. If you can't control your spending, go to a cash-only approach (which I'll explain later) and close the accounts, cut up the cards, and mail them back to the issuing bank. Credit card usage is a privilege that has great responsibilities.

I remember when my teenage daughter got her driver's license. I reminded her frequently that driving was a privilege and that when she was behind the wheel she had control of a dangerous weapon. Bad driving can kill people. I believe she took my counsel to heart, although I'm not shy to remind her, either. The same principle is at work with credit. It is a powerful tool in your financial and personal life. But if abused or used foolishly, it can lead to years of misery. Learn to use money wisely, no matter how much you participate in consumer credit.

GAIN GOD'S BLESSING THROUGH YOUR STRUGGLES

What will happen to your finances when you seek first the kingdom? Many passages give us insight into what we can expect God to do. Matthew 6:33 has already promised us "these things." Another passage that fits especially well is Deuteronomy 8:16–18. The parallels are amazingly similar, God's people were in the desert, literally. They had made big mistakes, but God still loved them. Miraculously, He provided them with water to drink and quail and manna to eat. He kept their shoes and clothing from wearing out (Deuteronomy 8:4). Even though the trek to the Promised Land would take forty years, God didn't give up on them. Here's what was going on:

> He gave you manna to eat in the desert, something your fathers had never known, to humble and to test you so that in the end it might go well with you. You may say to yourself, "My power and the strength of my hands have produced this wealth for me." But remember the LORD your God, for it is he who gives you the ability to produce wealth, and so confirms his covenant, which he swore to your forefathers, as it is today. (Deuteronomy 8:16-18)

To help the children of Israel really escape from the desert caused by their disobedience and poor decisions, God did three things:

1. He humbled them.
2. He tested them.
3. He did good for them.

HUMILITY AS A GREAT TEACHER

Humility is the key to all behavioral changes. If we don't have the humility to see the need for a change, we would have to believe we're perfect. That's obviously not the case for any of us. So what if you've blown it financially? What if you've made serious, foolish spending decisions? What if you are worried and struggling with the consequences of unwise debt? Join the crowd. No one has a perfect track record. Most of us have made plenty of financial mistakes, just like we've made lots of other mistakes. So don't beat yourself up for blowing it. Instead, embrace the humility to admit your mistakes and accept the fact that you can't fix these problems on your own. You need God and his mercy as well as the help and advice of trusted godly advisors in order to get back on track. This will completely disarm the enemies of inferiority and guilty feelings.

Humility means making new decisions, accepting new disciplines, and walking new paths that will gradually lead you to better results. All of us could stand a dose of humility on this topic, because even if you're doing a good job now, there's still room for improvement. Give some thought about spending less on some items and more on others. And if you are caught in the Debt Trap, try seeing your experience as a difficult lesson in what happens when using the world's economic philosophy and systems to accomplish your goals or escape the trap on your own.

Most financial ditches occur because of indulgent spending, and most overspending comes from a desire for more . . . and more . . . and more. The problem with more is that it's never enough. We've seen how the root problem is not actually buying or spending; it always goes back to the four enemies. Think about why you spend. Do you know the difference between true wants and needs? The lines in our culture have been blurred by modern marketing tactics. It can be as simple as the fast-food order taker asking, "Do you want the "Super Value Meal Deal" (as if the regular-sized meal isn't enough) or the commercials that imply that women will look as beautiful as a famous actress or model by using a certain brand of cosmetics or hair color.

Think about how easy it is to buy and spend and consume more and more with no apparent negative consequences. Too often it's only when the bank account is drained dry and the credit card debts are stacked high that the price of mistakes gets our attention long enough to let humility and conviction settle in.

Almost a hundred Bible verses involve humility. The opposite of proud, humility is a recognition that we don't have the answers. It works in tandem with conviction—it's a signal that we are ready for a change.

Guess what? This willingness to let God work is the invitation for him to start.

Several years ago I discovered a surprise blessing about humility. One of the most interesting verses in the Bible talks about this subject and ties it to Moses: "Now Moses was a very humble man, more humble than anyone else on the face of the earth." The story tells how Moses' brother Aaron and his sister Miriam had complained that God didn't limit his speaking to Moses. Their intent was clearly one of jealousy, too. So God came down in a pillar of cloud and spoke to them saying, "Listen to my words: 'When a prophet of the LORD is among you, I reveal myself to him in visions, I speak to him in dreams. But this is not true of my servant Moses; he is faithful in all my house. With him I speak face to face, clearly and not in riddles; he sees the form of the LORD. Why then were you not afraid to speak against my servant Moses?'" (Numbers 12:3, 6–8).

God was clearly ticked at their pride and honored Moses for his humility. Moses' humility and faithful response opened the door for God to communicate with him clearly. While no one should claim to be a prophet like Moses today, doesn't it make sense that we'll perceive God's wisdom and direction more clearly when we are truly humble?

Think of other ways God endorses and blesses humility:

> The LORD sends poverty and wealth; he humbles and he exalts. (1 Samuel 2:7)

> You save the humble, but your eyes are on the haughty to bring them low. (2 Samuel 2:28)

> If my people, who are called by my name, will humble themselves and pray and seek my face and turn from their wicked ways, then will I hear from heaven and will forgive their sin and will heal their land. (2 Chronicles 7:14)

> He guides the humble in what is right and teaches them his way. (Psalm 25:9)

> Before his downfall a man's heart is proud, but humility comes before honor. (Proverbs 18:12)

> Humility and the fear of the LORD bring wealth and honor and life. (Proverbs 22:4)

> He has showed you, O man, what is good. And what does the LORD require of you? To act justly and to love mercy and to walk humbly with your God. (Micah 6:8)

> For whoever exalts himself will be humbled, and whoever humbles himself will be exalted. (Matthew 23:12)

> But he gives us more grace. That is why Scripture says: "God opposes the proud but gives grace to the humble." (James 4:6)

> Humble yourselves, therefore, under God's mighty hand, that he may lift you up in due time. (1 Peter 5:6)

Do you think God wants your attention? In spite of your feelings of fear, guilt, resentment, or other related emotions, draw a line in the sand and make a decision. You can learn from your mistakes, trust God's ways, and believe in his power and goodness to get you out of your mess. Remember also that God isn't causing the pain and the problem. We are. But God will allow the struggle to get our attention. Then he can teach us new ways.

PASS THE TESTS

The biggest surprise to me in Deuteronomy 18:16–18 was the middle part of the passage. After God humbled the Israelites and before he blessed them, the Word says that "he tested them." This explains a lot. The humility caused by their plight was enough to get their attention and point them in the right direction, but before the changes would have a chance to settle in permanently, God tested them, too. This is the part that drives us crazy. When we repent and decide to change, there is something in our flesh that says we should get to start fresh. But, in our heart of hearts, don't we know that it takes time and effort to learn healthier and lasting behaviors?

This is true in all areas of life. It's only when we walk something out over time that we find lasting insight and genuine strength to overcome. Romans 5:3–5 says it this way, "We also rejoice in our sufferings, because we know that suffering produces perseverance; perseverance, character; and character, hope. And hope does not disappoint us, because God has poured out his love into our hearts by the Holy Spirit, whom he has given us." James 1:2–5 gives us another dose: "Consider it pure joy, my brothers, whenever you face trials of many kinds, because you know that the testing of your faith develops perseverance. Perseverance must finish its work so that you may be mature and complete, not lacking anything. If any of you lacks wisdom, he should ask God, who gives generously to all without finding fault, and it will be given to him."

Even if you have already begun making good financial decisions, perhaps you experienced a time of testing. God uses time and experiences to sow his truths and wisdom deeper and deeper into our hearts. I also believe the endurance gained through financial struggles will serve us well when we face other challenges in the future. We've already spent time understanding that the devil rolls out several schemes against us in his efforts to divorce us from our walk with God. You are now armed with knowledge—his approaches are now very predictable, even when the issues are quite different.

A TIME OF TESTING

As one of my friends likes to remind me, "When the student is taking a test, the teacher is quiet." While making your escape from the Debt Trap, expect a period of testing. Satan may attempt to stir up pain from past financial, legal, health, or relationship problems. But no matter why or what, every test is passed the same way—by trusting God. I've personally faced five major life-challenges so far, and God has been present through every one. Some of the challenges were my fault while some were not. But the peace and power that God brought and brings has been invaluable. Have you noticed that we typically don't learn a lot in the good times? The most powerful learning experiences occur during times of challenge—even when our disobedience has caused them. Remember the prodigal spender? Come on home—God is waiting for your return.

GET READY FOR GOOD

Praise the Lord for the last part of Deuteronomy 8:16. Remember what the Lord said? His plan is that "in the end it might go well with you." I love the good stuff God wants to do. But I'm ready for it only after humility and testing.

Take a look at these passages: Deuteronomy 4:40; 28:11–13; Joshua 1:8; Jeremiah 7:23; Psalm 62:11–12; 128:1–2; Proverbs 11:25; 13:21; Isaiah 61:8; Ephesians 6:1–3; 3 John 2.

I really enjoyed reading Deuteronomy 28:13 about God's people being the head and not the tail. Financial burdens clearly make you feel like the tail, don't they? That's why God's ways are the way to go. At the same time, never forget that the best rewards are so much better than money and material blessing.

Life, health, friendship, and faith bring true peace. The "stuff" may only add frustration and distraction. Several years ago, a good friend of ours was spending her devotional time in the Word and ran across this verse: "Why spend money on what is not bread, and your labor on what does not satisfy? Listen, listen to me, and eat what is good, and your soul will delight in the richest of fare" (Isaiah 55:2). She told us how convicting that verse was to her. She had been feeling that her shopping habits had gotten slightly out of hand. It wasn't that she was doing anything wrong, either, although her husband might disagree with me on this one. She sensed that her heavenly Father wanted her to grow to the next level in his wisdom. So when she read this verse it provided a gentle nudge back onto a path of more intently seeking the kingdom as her number-one passion.

Did you know God has a passion for us as well? That's why he sent Jesus, why he gives us guidance, why he counts the hairs on our heads, why he sings over us from heaven, why he rejoices when we come home to him, why he will send Jesus back for us, and so much more. So is it any wonder that he would also add "all these things," the daily necessities of life, to our lives? My passion, your passion, and our passion for God is because of what he did, does, and will do. It's not in order to get anything from him, at all. It's a simple focus, hard to sustain to be sure, but so well worth any cost.

So, seek first God's kingdom and his righteousness. We have his guarantee that he will give us everything we need to sustain us as we make our way free of the Debt Trap.

Then you will know the truth,
and the truth will set you free.

—JOHN 8:32

chapter four

The Escape Plan

IMAGINE STANDING in front of two doors. On one door is the sign "World Truth" and on the other, the sign "Jesus' Truth." Which truth has your best interests in mind? If you're thinking, "Jesus' Truth," good. That's what the escape plan is about. Let's apply John 8:31–32 to our finances. "To the Jews who had believed him, Jesus said, 'If you hold to my teaching, you are really my disciples. Then you will know the truth, and the truth will set you free.'" See the way it works? First we hold to Jesus' teaching about a topic. "Hold" means trust. In other words, take God at his word. Second, know the truth. "Know" implies both knowledge and application. Another word for this is wisdom. Then thirdly, this wisdom will "set us free." It will empower us to escape bondage.

One of the essential roles good parents play is to teach their children truth. A wise and loving father knows his children do better when they base their values, attitudes, and actions on what's right. Good parents support us when we mess up, but they also give us advice and instruction to get us back on the track to freedom. I'm grateful to have a mom and dad like that. And I am trying to do the same with my children.

Telling the truth is also one of the traits we can trust our heavenly Father to possess. God will always tell the truth, including the truth about finances. Even when we mess up through overspending or getting entangled in unwise debt, he will still love us, teach us, and support us as we learn and apply truth. There's something really powerful about a Father who never writes us off. This is God's nature. As the writer of Hebrews put it, "Keep your lives free from the love of money and be content with what you have, because God has said, 'Never will I leave you; never will I forsake you.' So we say with confidence, 'The Lord is my helper; I will not be afraid. What can man do to me?'" (Hebrews 13:5–6).

As we work with God to battle our debt, let's remember his promise. The Lord will be our helper. He will lead us through truth into freedom. This is important to remember. Sometimes, after we get into a financial mess, we think God will instantly bail us out as soon as we start trusting him and his ways. While he may deliver a great and amazing miracle, there can be more value to a gradual deliverance that leads us out of the debt desert step by step. He uses truth to teach us new ways and allows time to provide a structure for learning that will make it much harder for us to go back into bondage.

We've recognized the trap we're in, we've discovered the law of the harvest, received the guarantee of seeking first the kingdom, and now we're ready to learn how to make the escape. The truth really will set us free!

HOW TO GET OUT

The Debt Trap is easy to fall into, isn't it? Usually we don't know we're in it until we're surrounded by bills and swallowed up by fear and doubt. God never intended for us to live this way. So let's start right now and decide to escape the Debt

Trap. Follow this plan and you'll start seeing positive results in a short time:

1. *Determine why you're in debt.* Did habitual overspending catch up with you? Is your income suddenly too low? Leave the guilty feelings in the past. Simply determine the cause and come to grips with it.

2. *Stop going deeper into debt.* This is huge. Stop spending more than you earn. Before you can get well you have to stop the bleeding. Pay cash for all purchases. Be firm with yourself. You may have to cut up your cards to resist increasing your balance. Don't use credit cards as a stopgap measure, even if you've lost your job. Test every expenditure and allow no sacred cows. No expense is too small to ask the question, "Do I really need this right now?" Many legitimate purchases can be put off for a better time. See what expenses you can reduce or eliminate. This is tough, but it nets results.

3. *Find out how much you owe.* You need to know an exact amount so you can create a plan to pay it off. With a good plan and patience you can reverse your course, recover, and stay out of trouble. Resist opening up new credit card accounts. This will help you avoid a quickfix that many times turns disastrous.

4. *Know your income and expenses.* This will be much like a financial CAT scan! Although this diagnostic tool requires some time and effort, it will give you a clear picture of any problem areas. And it will provide insight into solutions. Even if you think you're in pretty good financial shape, discipline yourself to go through this process. We all have room to improve our fiscal well-being.

One of the things you'll need to do is to write down your financial goals, your income, your expenses, and so forth. You may want to use forms or worksheets developed by financial planners. Or you may simply use blank, lined paper—it's low-tech, but it works just the same. The main objective is to write down what you're doing and compare it to what you need to do.

(Note: If you would like to use professional worksheets, you can find them online at www.escapethedebttrap.com or by calling 1-800-364-5665, or you may ask your minister.)

Gather all the documents you need to complete your worksheets. It will resemble doing your taxes, so take your time. This time investment is crucial to your financial well-being now and especially for the future. I'd suggest getting out your calendar and making deadlines for gathering data and then carefully completing each worksheet.

Date and file these worksheets. If you'll update them at least annually, it will be like taking an annual physical. You'll see your progress and be able to see if any corrections are needed. Then, whenever you consider purchases for the future, you can more easily count the cost—the principle Jesus spoke of in Luke 14:28–30. It should also pay off when you prepare your federal income taxes. If you are inclined to work through this process on a monthly basis, my hat is off to you. It takes great discipline, but it is truly the best way to keep up with your financial health and strength.

Most people think that if they have money in their checkbook at the end of the month, they must be okay. However, debt from unsecured credit cards can creep up gradually, greatly increasing your monthly expenses! Approximately 25 percent of the people with credit card debt report that they're paying only the minimum amount. That is a recipe for disaster! If you're paying only the monthly minimum on your card (or cards) but are still making new purchases, you will see your payments increase quickly. Remember that even if the minimum payment amount is printed on your statement or if the bankcard company offers to let you skip a month, the interest keeps accumulating on all unpaid balances.

5. *Make a spending plan.* This is a multistep plan. Your objective is to figure out how to spend only what you must so you can dedicate as much as possible to a debt repayment plan, savings plan, and a giving plan. Savings plans will eventually be segmented into savings for retirement, education, emergencies, repair, and replacement. It may not be a large amount in the beginning, but with a well-prepared spending plan, your reserves will grow in time.

Now comes the dreaded "B" word: BUDGET. Most of us hate to think of budgeting because it implies restriction. But we do need a plan. Whether it's a plan for eating or spending, the best plans net the best results. The better the strategies in our plan, the more effective our use of money will be. Completing your financial worksheets guides you through this process.

So let's put it together by making a list of all your expenses on a spending analysis worksheet. First, it is essential to realize you need to spend less than your income. Secondly, determine true needs and begin to establish some goals to adjust your spending so that your money goes first to your priorities. Referring to your list of monthly expenses, it will be like working a jigsaw puzzle. You'll have to pull some funds from one place to another in order to create the right picture. As you lay out your plan, be sure to use a pencil on this worksheet! Start with your regular fixed expenses (giving to the Lord's work, mortgage or rent, car, insurance). Now consider monthly expenses where the amount varies from month to month such as groceries, utilities, even taxes. Sometimes you'll need to use an annual total and divide by twelve to obtain a monthly average. Carefully prioritize additional expenses and commitments. Giving to the Lord's work, buying a house, and saving for your child's education and your own retirement is more important than going to the movies or eating out. Plan inexpensive recreation, too. Just remember that you are looking for ways to free up cash to apply to your debt reduction worksheet. Watch how much you spend. Think long term as you look for ways to contain your spending. Another powerful way to contain your expenses is to get a receipt or record for every purchase you make during the week. No expense is too small. Make sure these weekly expenses are included on your spending analysis worksheet. Add up the week's receipts and see what you got for your money. Is the morning coffee on the way to work worth an extra ten dollars or more a week?

Now you are ready to take the information from the analysis and create a written plan, your true budget. You started with two major objectives: spend less than you make, and tie all spending to your priorities. When God is first, it will show up in your spending. That's not to say your giving will be the biggest item in your spending plan, although it might be. It simply means you have intentionally matched your actions with your goals. You can put this into practice by writing your checks according to the *priority* of the expense rather than by the *amount* of the expense. The most important checks are written first: giving, house payment, other budgeted necessities. The other items and decisions come later.

6. *Develop a written repayment plan.* Your top priority in this repayment plan will be your secured assets. These are the items you will lose to the lender if you don't repay in time. Your next priority is to repay the debt on unsecured purchases. The plan may take you longer to fulfill, but typically these lenders

are more willing to work with you—especially if you're working with a financial counselor.

Consider doubling up on your payments. This is possible if you have cut back on your discretionary spending in your written budget. Eat out less often. Buy less expensive items. Make what you wear and use last longer. Whatever you decide to do, write it down and keep your written budget near your bills. This will help you remember to keep finding money to put toward your repayment plan.

Another way of attacking debt is to take your smaller balances and pay them off first. You will gain both the satisfaction of checking it off the list of liabilities and applying that amount toward remaining debts or your emergency reserves.

7. *Develop a savings plan.* As mentioned earlier in step 5, spending and saving need to work in tandem. If you haven't already done this, you need to develop a savings plan with short-term and long-range objectives. One place to focus your short-term savings is on an "uh-oh fund." This is money you will definitely need when something breaks. Save until you've put $1,000 in this fund. You will feel a great deal of satisfaction and relief when you have the cash reserves to handle that next maintenance emergency.

After establishing your emergency fund, prioritize your long-term goals. Even if you have only now begun to save, it's better late than never. And remember, once you have settled all of your balances on your repayment plan, you can devote more money to saving and giving. Seek godly counsel on the most profitable ways to save and invest for the future.

8. *Set goals.* Now that you've gone through the first steps of immediate damage control and begun at least a modest savings plan, start concentrating on money management. It begins by

setting good financial goals—both short term and long term. The process will serve to crystallize your thinking. Even if you can set aside only one dollar a month toward your goals, do that! It will create a concrete goal instead of a fuzzy one. As you pay off old debts, apply that money to your goal accounts. If you want to put your kids through college, buy a home, tithe, support mission work, or pay off debt, you must concretely establish that objective.

Goal setting is important when buying a house. When we bought our first house we were planning to begin our family in two or three years, so we looked for a house that my salary alone could handle. We obviously wanted a house in a safe neighborhood and close to my workplace. And we wanted a place where we could invite people from church over for fellowship. We had all these ideas in mind, and God led us to a wonderful house. Given our stage in life, it was exactly what we wanted. We were even able to get a special, lower interest rate on the home because we were first-time homeowners. If you have home ownership as one of your goals, getting your debt load under control will help you make this possible.

A noted national speaker and author Stephen Covey says, "Begin with the end in sight." That's the essence of good goal setting. Jesus taught the importance of counting the cost:

> Suppose one of you wants to build a tower. Will he not first sit down and estimate the cost to see if he has enough money to complete it? For if he lays the foundation and is not able to finish it, everyone who sees it will ridicule him, saying, "This fellow began to build and was not able to finish." Or suppose a king is about to go to war against another king. Will he not first sit down and consider whether he is able with ten thousand men to oppose the one

> coming against him with twenty thousand? If he is not able, he will send a delegation while the other is still a long way off and will ask for terms of peace. In the same way, any of you who does not give up everything he has cannot be my disciple. "Salt is good, but if it loses its saltiness, how can it be made salty again?" (Luke 14:28–34)

When we approach more spending decisions by starting with the goals, we make better decisions about homes, cars, college, retirement, and so forth. A serendipity to goal setting is becoming less vulnerable to impulse buying and more focused on the future.

When we're dealing with money and finance issues, it is similar to going to war. We have resources and we have enemies. To win the battles, we'll need to calculate literally what we need to be successful and victorious.

Once our thinking on spending is determined by our goals, it affects our motivation. We will see the long haul, believe in our direction, and find encouragement in the tough decisions. It's easier to stay on target when we have hope.

Once we have our goals in mind, our spending priorities will follow. As mentioned earlier, we can determine our spending priorities very simply by looking at the order in which we write the checks. So if God is first in our life, our offering check will be the first, not the last check we write each week. Next might come our house or rent payment. Go down the line, based on priorities. If paying off debt or increasing your level of giving is a priority, you won't just say it; you'll do something about it! Get that amount written as high in the payment list as you can. Make it a commitment as important as any other, and don't forget it.

9. *Keep simple, accurate records.* Simply follow the plan you make. It is important to examine your bank statement and

balance your checkbook, too. I read a CNN poll indicating that 40 percent of Americans don't balance their checkbooks. This can be especially crucial if you use an ATM for cash or if you use a debit card for purchases. My wife balances our checkbook. She discovered we had a $792 discrepancy between the checkbook register and the amount actually in the bank. It was a simple mistake on our part, too. The bank didn't cause the problem; I did. I paid a number of household bills online and left my wife the records so she could put them in the register. Somehow these papers were misplaced. Thank goodness, since my wife regularly balances the checkbook, she caught the problem before our account was overdrawn.

There's no doubt about it, the record-keeping side of financial management can be tedious. If this feels too burdensome, yet you know you need help, you can also try using the envelope system for spending. This is one of the oldest but most efficient ways to keep your spending under control without having to watch and analyze lots of receipts. The envelope system works this way: Label separate envelopes for each category of expense you're trying to control. At the start of each month or pay period, place enough cash in each envelope to cover your planned spending. For example, you might have envelopes for groceries, recreation, clothing, eating out, etc. When you're headed to the store, check to see how much money you have in the envelope. If you have enough to cover your planned purchases, go for it. Just remember that the amount in the envelope has to cover you until you get paid again and can refill the envelope. If you don't have enough money, you can pull money from one of the other envelopes. If you decide to buy movie tickets instead of groceries, that's your choice.

This approach is sometimes criticized because people worry about having too much cash laying around. I don't recommend it for fixed or committed expenses, only discretionary spending areas. Keep the money in a secure place and when you have money leftover—don't spend it! Place the extra money in a savings account. You'll be pleased at how your spending will go down naturally when you rely more on cash than the convenience of credit cards or even cash cards.

10. *Practice good money management.* When you start taking these steps, you'll be in the position of practicing good management skills. The challenge is to stay on track. As the saying goes, plan your work and work your plan. God's Word makes it clear that God owns and oversees everything (Psalm 50:10; Deuteronomy 8:17–18; Jeremiah 27:5; 32:17; Ephesians 1:1). We are actually his managers of these resources (Luke 16:10–13). So it follows that we need to constantly employ good management skills to use and master. If you're in the Debt Trap, these skills will help you get out. Once you're free of the Debt Trap, the following steps will play a major role in keeping you free.

STAYING FREE

The important step toward true freedom is remembering the truth of Jesus' comments in Matthew 16:24–26: Then Jesus said to his disciples, "If anyone would come after me, he must deny himself and take up his cross and follow me. For whoever wants to save his life will lose it, but whoever loses his life for me will find it. What good will it be for a man if he gains the whole world, yet forfeits his soul? Or what can a man give in exchange for his soul?" Nothing is more valuable than your soul and the souls of the people you love. It's significant that Jesus uses the phrase "gains the whole world." He's using financial terminology to tell us that our lives are an investment.

As we formulate our personal plans to escape debt, we have an opportunity to take stock of our lives. How are we investing our lives in our family, friends, and opportunities to influence our coworkers, neighbors, and others? Are we making a difference for the kingdom of God?

The amount of money we have doesn't correlate to happiness. In fact, the more we have, the harder it can be to enjoy and appreciate our blessings. I believe this is one of the reasons why Paul said he had learned how to be content. It never comes naturally or automatically. "I am not saying this because I am in need, for I have learned to be content whatever the circumstances. I know what it is to be in need, and I know what it is to have plenty. I have learned the secret of being content in any and every situation, whether well fed or hungry, whether living in plenty or in want" (Philippians 4:11–12).

AVOID FINANCIAL TEMPTATION

By understanding the importance of living contented lives that are based on following Jesus, we become empowered to handle the pitfalls of temptation! Satan will undoubtedly resort to any tactics he can to challenge our new way of thinking. Diligence is the key to staying free from the temptations that could lure us back into the Debt Trap.

GUARD AGAINST GREEDY DESIRES

One day a man came to Jesus arguing about how to divide an inheritance with his brother. Jesus said, "Watch out! Be on your guard against all kinds of greed; a man's life does not consist in the abundance of his possessions" (Luke 12:15).

The desire for possessions is not automatically a bad desire. After all, we can't live without food, clothes, and shelter. Cars, appliances, and office equipment allow us to use our time and energy more efficiently, and other possessions can make life more enjoyable. It's when this desire gets twisted by the devil that it becomes a problem. We may think we fell into the Debt Trap by accident. We didn't. An evil being the Bible calls Satan, lured us away from safety. We should recognize there was nothing accidental about our mistakes. While our guard was down, we fell for the trap set for us by a very intelligent and powerful enemy who's been at this for a very long time. So, since he is working to bring us down, we should find a defensive position to guard against greedy desires.

James 1:14–15 says, "Each one is tempted when, by his own evil desire, he is dragged away and enticed. Then, after desire has conceived, it gives birth to sin; and sin, when it is full-grown, gives birth to death." Although we may not be totally at fault for our past financial blunders, we are now responsible for making better decisions and for learning to overcome the consequences. So rather than let guilty feelings beat us down, let God build us up. Ask for his insight when confronted by the tricks of greed.

RESIST THE LIES, HALF-TRUTHS, AND TRICKS

Knowing that we need clothes to wear and a place to live, Satan can whisper in your ear, *That's not good enough for you* (lie). *You deserve a better home* (half-truth). *You should get it if you can* (trick). So we buy or lease more house than we can afford. Uh-oh, we're several steps deeper in the Debt Trap. Or he might tempt us by leading us to look in our closet and say, "Is this all I have [lie]? Nothing looks good on me [half-truth]. I don't want my friends to think I don't have any style [half-truth]." So we head for the store, pull out the plastic, and calm our nerves with spending. Oops. Another step or two into the Debt Trap. See how we were set up? It's easy to fall into the trap.

This list of items we might choose to purchase is endless. Our backgrounds, friendship circles, and personal tastes and preferences all vary widely. Sometimes a person's income is high enough to keep them out of major trouble longer than someone else. But let's not be deceived. If anything, wealthier people often get into a deeper trap because their appetite for possessions and a good time causes them to spend more rapidly. A steady combination of lies, half-truths, and tricks, comes at us relentlessly. Decide in advance how you are going to deal with these lies and half-truths before they pop up. Predetermine your route of escape and then stick to your plan.

Colossians 3:5 says, "Put to death, therefore, whatever belongs to your earthly nature: sexual immorality, impurity, lust, evil desires and greed, which is idolatry." Several key ideas stand out relating this verse to the Debt Trap. But the idea that comes through the strongest is the use of the word *greed.* What a creepy word! Who ever feels personally guilty of this? Instead, we tend to save this word to describe a self-absorbed and uncaring corporate executive.

In reality, all of us are prey to greed because its root meaning is simply "a desire for more." Whether we have a lot or a little, if our focus is always to get more and never be content or satisfied, we covet.

Many times I've told my children, and myself, that if you can't enjoy things when you have a little, you'll never enjoy having a lot. How can that be? Because no matter how much we have, if we constantly want more, the devil's dart has penetrated our hearts. Instead, take this word to heart: "I know what it is to be in need, and I know what it is to have plenty. I have learned the secret of being content in any and every situation, whether well fed or hungry, whether living in plenty or in want. I can do everything through him who gives me strength" (Philippians 4:12–13). The apostle Paul said the ability to be content and enjoy what we have right now can be *learned* from God. See him as the source of our blessing, seek his wisdom, trust his provision, and you'll sidestep this dart most of the time.

If we don't check our desire for more (greed), we'll be suckers for the slick and persuasive ad campaigns on the radio, TV, billboards, and print media. We'll think, *I have to have that.* Easy credit makes impulse spending possible, but the total debt load creeps up on us quickly. We open the credit card statement and look immediately at the total we owe. After a gulp (or a scream), we immediately look at the individual transactions, hoping the bank or merchant made a series of huge mistakes. Unfortunately, they seldom do. We really owe that much. We spent a few bucks at one place, a few more at another. We note that we never spent a lot at any one store, either. So what happened? Easy. We forgot to ask some very basic questions: Was this item a need or a want? Did I have to buy it now? Can I afford it? Could I have bought it less expensively somewhere else? What will I give up to allow me to make this purchase?

That might be a lot of questions to ask, but we can learn to remember them if we want to change and escape badly enough. Read these verses of wisdom: "Of what use is money in the hand of a fool, since he has no desire to get wisdom?" (Proverbs 17:16). "Whoever loves money never has money enough; whoever loves wealth is never satisfied with his income. This too is meaningless. . . . Wisdom is a shelter as money is a shelter, but the advantage of knowledge is this: that wisdom preserves the life of its possessor" (Ecclesiastes 5:10; 7:12).

Proverbs 13:7 speaks directly to this issue: "One man pretends to be rich, yet has nothing; another pretends to be poor, yet has great wealth." Often we buy to make it look like we're "doing well." In reality, our finances may be a wreck. On the other hand, the people who appear to be poor often have money saved up for the times they need it the most.

Have you heard Oseola McCarty's amazing story? Miss McCarty spent her entire working career washing and ironing clothes for the townspeople of Hattiesburg, Mississippi, home of the University of Southern Mississippi. She gave to her local church, paid her bills, saved her money, and lived a simple but comfortable life. When she retired at the age of eighty-six, she checked with her banker to see how much money was in her account. She discovered that her life's savings had slowly and quietly grown to $250,000. She determined to give $150,000 of the total to the University of Southern Mississippi because, "I want to help somebody's child go to college." Her banker, Paul Laughlin, said, "She seems wonderfully at peace with where she is and who she is." Miss McCarty passed away in 1999 at the age of ninety-one, but through her generosity, her legacy will live on forever.

AVOID MAKING ASSUMPTIONS

Life, after all, is a series of good experiences and challenges. Our finances are the same way. Leave yourself some breathing room in your spending decisions and their resultant payment obligations. Don't assume that you'll always have the same level of income. This may sound obvious when thinking about a house or a car. But it's also important when thinking about less expensive decisions that, when taken together, can add up to becoming a huge chunk of our monthly obligations. More and more people are committed to contracts for cable TV, cell phones, memberships, and other useful but nonessential services. Avoid new contracts where possible. Scale back or renegotiate reduced plans. When considering big-ticket purchases, think long and hard about your ability to pay them off if you lose your job, get sick or disabled, or have unexpected repair bills or medical expenses.

When buying something using a credit card, you are signing an agreement to pay for that item or service. It is in fact a loan, too.

So, think twice before committing to new obligations, and have a plan to meet them should your income decrease. As Christians we have a fundamental commitment to keep these promises if at all possible. Psalm 37:21 says, "The wicked borrow and do not repay, but the righteous give generously." If we do make a commitment to repay a lender, let's make it a priority to repay on a set time frame. As the apostle Paul put it, "Let no debt remain outstanding, except the continuing debt to love one another, for he who loves his fellowman has fulfilled the law" (Romans 13:8). That means debt, by itself, is not wrong, but letting a debt become outstanding is. Paying back on time will help you stay on track and out of the trap.

RECOGNIZING VULNERABILITIES

Early on we established that our foundation for getting free starts with changing how we think and believe. After we know where we have been vulnerable to financial temptations, we can establish the following wisdom principles to reflect our new goals and stay free:

> Lazy hands make a man poor, but diligent hands bring wealth. (Proverbs 10:4)
>
> Whoever trusts in his riches will fall. (Proverbs 11:28)
>
> A wise son heeds his father's instruction, but a mocker does not listen to rebuke. (Proverbs 13:1)
>
> Do not be a man who strikes hands in pledge or puts up security for debts; if you lack the means to pay, your very bed will be snatched from under you. (Proverbs 22:26–27)

These and similar passages in other parts of the Bible empower me to fight financial temptations when I follow their wise counsel:

- Be honest. This is the bedrock for all financial dealings (2 Kings 12:15).

- Live within your means. Don't spend more than you make. This one principle will protect you most of the time from the Debt Trap (Proverbs 15:16).
- Give an honest day's work for an honest day's wages. You'll get better jobs, higher income, and more people who respect you (Colossians 3:23).
- Help others. God's plan is that money and possessions be used for higher purposes than to simply consume them yourself (Hebrews 13:16).

This action is both defensive and offensive. Think of Satan as a finance terrorist in our lives who wants to destroy our financial health because it gives him access to other areas of our life. Defend yourself vigilantly against this stealthy enemy. But at the same time you're on the defensive, grab the offensive and focus on positive principles.

TRUST AND OBEY

Trust the Lord's teachings and then consistently apply them. Freedom is obtained and maintained as you do both. Trust God's help as you fight the urge to be double-minded as you're being tossed by winds of the world's way one time and then God's way the next. Your faithful consistency and patience will keep you from returning to the clutches of the Debt Trap. The rewards of freedom and peace are guaranteed.

His master replied, “Well done, good
and faithful servant! You have been
faithful with a few things; I will
put you in charge of many things.
Come and share your master’s
happiness.”

—MATTHEW 25:21

chapter five

The Reward

ONE OF THE BEST business books I've ever read is *The Seven Habits of Highly Effective People* by Steven Covey. Among the nuggets of wisdom is this: "Begin with the end in sight." This is a fabulous life principle that fits easily into our financial planning. Experience tells me that this may be the number-one reason why we don't make every effort to stay financially healthy. Perhaps we make too many short-term financial decisions. We buy for the here and now, rather than save, invest, and give toward the future. It's far too easy to buy now and pay later, and later, and later. Few of us realize how much better it is to set aside funds for the future and make conservative spending plans.

It reminds me a lot of the reason why our physical health as a nation is in decline. Rather than exercise, watch our diet, and pay attention to nutrition to prevent disease, we wait until there's a problem, and then we'll do anything and pay everything for the cure. An article by Dr. Kenneth Cooper, one of the all-time great gurus in preventive medicine, mentions that his colleagues advised against his developing a medical practice around prevention. "You see, preventive medicine was viewed as the 'Cinderella' of the medical community. How could a young doctor come to town and expect to earn a living by keeping people well? I was told time and time again, 'There's no profit in the prevention of disease, only in the treatment of disease'"[1]

Dr. Cooper went ahead with his plans and has contributed greatly to the growing interest in the field of preventive medicine. And while this effort is now at an all-time high, most Americans still don't make many substantial changes in their level of physical activity until a major physical emergency lights up on their mental dashboard. Why is it that we wait until a problem occurs before we decide to change? Why must we wait for a big problem before we wake up to the long-term reality?

As the old maxim goes, an ounce of prevention is worth a pound of cure. What's true about physical diet and exercise is also true about financial spending and planning. Don't wait until you get around to it to make changes. One of these days we will all have the opportunity to stand before the Lord and hear him say, "Well done, good and faithful servant." I *want* to hear God say this to me—not just about my spiritual life but about the kind of husband and father I've been, about the kind of neighbor and worker I've been, about the kind of ministry influence I've been, and even about the way I've managed all of the resources he's given me. This includes money. In a very real sense, my money is God's money (Psalm 50:10) and God's money is my money (Acts 5:14).

Since this is true, I am eager to learn how to do the best job I can with my finances so I'll be one of the people God is truly proud of. What greater reward could we imagine? He is my loving heavenly father and my great God, so it blesses me to honor him.

As we look at "beginning with the end in sight" let me take you to the classic passage on this subject: Matthew 25:14–30.

This passage is filled with insights and gives tremendous motivation for living in the here and now in the light of eternity. If you and I can learn the words of the master in this passage and engrave them on our hearts, they will show us how to get out of the Debt Trap and stay out.

> Again, it will be like a man going on a journey, who called his servants and entrusted his property to them. To one he gave five talents of money, to another two talents, and to another one talent, each according to his ability. Then he went on his journey. The man who had received the five talents went at once and put his money to work and gained five more. So also, the one with the two talents gained two more. But the man who had received the one talent went off, dug a hole in the ground and hid his master's money.
>
> After a long time the master of those servants returned and settled accounts with them. The man who had received the five talents brought the other five. "Master," he said, "you entrusted me with five talents. See, I have gained five more."
>
> His master replied, "Well done, good and faithful servant! You have been faithful with a few things; I will put you in charge of many things. Come and share your master's happiness!"
>
> The man with the two talents also came. "Master," he said, "you entrusted me with two talents; see, I have gained two more."
>
> His master replied, "Well done, good and faithful servant! You have been faithful with a few things; I will put you in charge of many things. Come and share your master's happiness!"

> Then the man who had received the one talent came. "Master," he said, "I knew that you are a hard man, harvesting where you have not sown and gathering where you have not scattered seed. So I was afraid and went out and hid your talent in the ground. See, here is what belongs to you."
>
> His master replied, "You wicked, lazy servant! So you knew that I harvest where I have not sown and gather where I have not scattered seed? Well then, you should have put my money on deposit with the bankers, so that when I returned I would have received it back with interest.
>
> "Take the talent from him and give it to the one who has the ten talents. For everyone who has will be given more, and he will have an abundance. Whoever does not have, even what he has will be taken from him. And throw that worthless servant outside, into the darkness, where there will be weeping and gnashing of teeth." (Matthew 25:14–30)

"WELL DONE"—WHAT WE WANT TO HEAR

The first phrase the master speaks to the first two servants, following their successful use of the funds that were entrusted to them is "well done." I love that phrase! It's what we hope to hear from a teacher when we get a test or paper back. It's what we want to hear from an employer when we find out how well we did on a project at work. And it is ultimately what we want to hear God say to us about our lives. Imagine God examining your financial circumstances and decisions right now. Could he and would he say, "Well done"? If not, don't despair. God wants you to pass every test and overcome every temptation you face. He is on your side. Rather than let the devil attack you with guilt, once again let these words warm your heart and give you a new target. If we will follow his lead, we will escape the Debt Trap. Seek him first, sow good financial seed, apply the truths and wisdom that will set you free, and patiently walk your way out. Look for God to open miraculous doors of blessing, affirmation, and provision. The process of having God become your financial planner will revolutionize your life.

I'll go one step further. If you will take the first step with God out of financial bondage, even that one first step will be all God waits for to begin whispering to your heart, *well done.* He longs to reward you with encouragement. Now—not just later. Take step after step, looking toward him all the way and he will be pleased.

"GOOD"—WHAT WE WANT TO BE

The next word the two honored servants heard was that they were good servants. The word *good* speaks to the quality of servants they were. In this passage, good is directly opposite to being wicked and lazy (verse 26). Other passages give more detail to this theme. There's the concept of good fruit (Matthew 3:10), which leads me to say good results in financial issues. There's the idea of *good* meaning worthwhile and useful (Matthew 5:13) versus good for nothing. I also note Jesus' teaching about letting the world see our good works and give the glory to God (Matthew 5:16). We want basic, positive, beneficial results to come from our handling of finances. So our desire in the financial arena is to be good in our use of resources—not just for us to be good *at* managing our use of money, credit, debt, or other financial tools. We can aspire to be good in and throughout all these applications. Goodness refers to our character, honesty, integrity, hard work, love, and concern as we apply financial management principles. For example, if I'm a good financial servant, I will see passages like Psalm 37:23–27 as my "marching orders." Look at how this scripture fits us, even if we're in the Debt Trap, perhaps even worried about our next meal:

> If the Lord delights in a man's way, he makes his steps firm; though he stumble, he will not fall, for the Lord upholds him with his hand. I was young and now I am old, yet I have never seen the righteous forsaken or their children begging bread. They are always generous and lend freely; their children will be blessed. Turn from evil and do good; then you will dwell in the land forever.

Isn't that great? God watches and works and waits for us to catch a glimpse of his vision. When we apply his standard of goodness to our finances, we build in protection against Satan's other schemes.

I like the way the *Good News Bible* translates Proverbs 3:7–8: "Never let yourself think that you are wiser than you are; simply obey the Lord and refuse to do wrong. If you do, it will be like good medicine, healing your wounds and easing your pains." That's a bonus reward! So when we aren't sure what the best thing to do is, we can *refuse to do the wrong thing.* How many bad decisions would we avoid if we follow this counsel? One time when talking to a friend of mine who is a CPA and company controller for a manufacturing and installation company, I asked him what he thought about a business deal I'd heard about. He said that it didn't pass "the smell test." He felt that while it might not be wrong, something about it "smelled" odd. And when the time came to explain it to others on the outside, there would be many questions, to say the least. It may sound obvious but, unfortunately far too many of us are falling short here. The bottom line is this: always tell the truth. Be who you say you are and do what you say you'll do. That is true integrity. That's the essence of being good. God knows that on our own we'll never attain sinless perfection. Without Christ's sacrifice, we'd all be toast. He simply wants the fabric of our lives to reflect his nature. Since he is the only one who is truly good (Matthew 19:7), our aim is to be like him as much as we can.

"FAITHFUL"—AN ACTION WORD

The two servants were also commended for their faithful actions. These qualities define our faithfulness, and they fit the context of this passage: trustworthy, dedicated, consistent, and able to handle more.

These qualities would fit any expression of faithfulness, but they are especially suited to our finances.

- Trustworthy—When we receive credit, the bank deems us as creditworthy and trusts us to pay back anything we borrow.
- Dedicated—Seeing God as our master causes us to dedicate our spending to his purposes. That protects us from foolish and harmful purchases (1 Timothy 6:9).
- Consistent—To get out of debt, we must stick to our escape plan. Plus, to build financial stability and strength for the future we will acquire the habit of saving and spending carefully, month after month, year after year.
- Able to handle more—If we want more authority, we have to be responsible for what we have and what is

currently under our control. In company finances, no one is promoted to handle larger sums until they prove they can handle the smaller amounts. As we get out of the Debt Trap, we can expect God to give us new opportunities in incremental steps. We'll get better as we go and learn to handle more with practice.

Another concept to consider is not specifically indicated in this passage. It is the idea of passing along what we have learned and are in the process learning. In 2 Timothy 2:2 Paul tells his young preacher friend, "And the things you have heard me say in the presence of many witnesses entrust to reliable men who will also be qualified to teach others." Some translations use "faithful" instead of "reliable." So perhaps one of the traits of a faithful servant is the willingness and the skills to show others. Not only are many adults reaping a bad harvest from their financial decisions, teenagers and children in our culture are growing up with almost no sense of healthy money management. As the credit card merchants gear up to create more debt, some of them deliberately target young people, knowing they lack the wisdom and discipline to say no when they shop, or the skills to use credit carefully. Many of these unsuspecting folks confuse having a credit card with knowing how to use it wisely. When they get in trouble, they turn to parents or friends to bail them out.

I believe that God wants all of us to make teaching others his principles of money management a priority. We must especially include training our children and grandchildren. If our loved ones are in the Debt Trap, he would certainly desire that we learn more and encourage them to get out too. The process of learning and experiencing financial freedom God's way could also be the path the Lord uses to build a strong, dynamic faith both in you and between you.

I encourage you to reach out to others in your congregation, neighborhood, or community. If you've learned how to manage your money effectively, you've earned both the right and responsibility to help others. Plus, if you've struggled to escape the Debt Trap and are making progress toward freedom, you should also think about giving your time and insight to help others who are where you were. If you've ever helped someone else overcome or succeed, you know how rewarding that feels.

I had an opportunity to visit with a single woman at church who has made major progress in her journey to get out of the Debt Trap. I planted a seed in her mind and heart to consider becoming a financial crisis helper someday soon. She looked at me as if I were crazy and said, "How can I help people when I have had such a hard time?" I told her that her sympathy and growing expertise would be exactly what some people would need. Remember, God never throws anyone on the scrap heap. He redeems us from problems and pains and gives us a ministry of serving others based on our deliverance.

"SERVANT"—HOW YOU GET IT DONE

If we're really wanting to hear God say, "Well done" to us, one of the roles we'll willingly embrace is that of a servant. Have you ever noticed how negative our feelings are when this word is used? I've participated in numerous business seminars on customer service. One of the eye openers is to ask people what they think of when they hear the word *servant.* People typically react with a frown or a negative tone and respond with "menial," "low pay," "entry level," and so forth. Yet, what kind of company would devalue serving or tending to the needs of its customers? A company in trouble! As soon as I figure out that serve means "work to add value for someone else," I will begin to see service as an honorable effort. In that context, we might all begin to see service as one of the highest professions in the world. In fact, some of the strongest businesses in the world today have made their mark by emphasizing service. Companies like Nordstrom, FedEx, and others thrive because of this commitment. Why not see God's business the same way? Our lives are a work in progress for God's use. This mission statement transforms our whole outlook and shifts our approach to finances into high gear. Have you wondered why Jesus called the third servant lazy? It is truly laughable to mention "servant" and "lazy" in the same sentence—an excellent oxymoron! He called him lazy because his feeble effort was valueless. This man added *nothing* to the resources God entrusted to him. It's as if the man never existed.

When we're God's servant in financial matters, our money is a tool to be used for kingdom purposes. This will require discipline (Proverbs 10:17) to follow my Master's desires to be a worker for him and make a difference. It's truly a reward to be honored as a servant of God because what he wants done is worth doing. Financially, I want the money I spend to make a positive impact rather than be valueless. What a waste! Timothy adds this bonus reward: "If a man cleanses himself from the latter, he will be an instrument for noble purposes, made holy, useful to the Master and prepared to do any good work" (2 Timothy 2:21).

It's also an honor to be his servant because he will care for us in the midst of our work (Philippians 4:19). Most of all, we want to be God's servant because when we're faithful servants, we get to be something else—his friend. Jesus said, "Greater love has no one than this, that he lay down his life for his friends. You are my friends if you do what I command. I no longer call you servants, because a servant does not know his master's business. Instead, I have called you friends, for everything that I learned from my Father I have made known to you" (John 15:13–15). Service leads to friendship. So God's plan for us, even in financial matters, is for us to see his business as our business, too.

One of our friends is a senior vice president of a major bank. He says that his company's corporate culture is summed up in the phrase "Run it like it's your own." His superiors want him to make decisions based on this policy and have given him enormous latitude in using his best judgment with company funds. I enjoyed seeing the excitement and commitment in his eyes as he talked about this responsibility. I know he is a good, faithful servant in that field and that he's doing a great job to extend the positive impact of his employer. If this attitude is expected in a bank, think about how much God must want it to be true in our lives? Every dollar God entrusts to your hands is one he wants to entrust to a friend. True friends don't waste the money, time, effort, opportunities, or any other valuable resource of another friend. If anything, they may even be more careful, because they know the friendship is more important than the funds.

Let's serve God the same way—as friends.

"COME AND SHARE THE BLESSINGS"—TRUE REWARDS

Escaping from the Debt Trap is neither easy nor fun. But if you'll get started, pay the price, and find some help along the way, the rewards far outweigh the struggle. Remember, if you're in the Debt Trap, you're going to have it rough either way. Would you rather have a hard time that gets even harder? That's the only result we have to look forward to if we don't make changes *right now.* Don't expect to find the pot of gold at the end of the rainbow. And for sure, don't go out and buy a lottery ticket, hoping to pay off your debts. I heard about the man in West Virginia who won $170 million in the state lottery who talked about giving a tenth of it to his church. I immediately hoped that no one uses this story to get others to think that God is leading them to buy a lottery ticket. That's no way to live. And a young man approached me at church a few years ago and told me that he was thinking of going to the horse track to place a bet to see if he could win enough money to pay off some of his bills. I couldn't believe how serious he was!

Please don't let the struggle from your experience in the Debt Trap entice you to either do nothing or do something goofy. Instead, let that same struggle and discomfort provide the energy for you to do whatever it takes to let you experience the blessings.

God has so many blessings he wants to reward us with as we escape the Debt Trap and walk in freedom. Here are only a few:

- Contentment (1 Timothy 6:6–9)
- Freedom from many griefs (1 Timothy 6:10)
- Harvest of righteousness (2 Corinthians 9:11)
- Abundance (Proverbs 3:9–10)
- Peace (Isaiah 26:3)
- The Lord's personal affirmation (Mark 10:29–31)

I especially appreciate 1 Timothy 6:6 which says, "But godliness with contentment is great gain." The phrase "great gain" is a synonym for "true wealth." When we put God's ways first and learn to enjoy what we have, we have a huge return on our investment. As the writer of Hebrews puts it, "So do not throw away your confidence; it will be richly rewarded. You need to persevere so that when you have done the will of God, you will receive what he has promised" (Hebrews 10:35–36).

Your confidence in man and the systems of the world will *always* let you down. It may come in the form of higher interest rates, downsizing, or a weak economy. Today's boom is tomorrow's bust. Haven't we learned this at last? I hope we have.

Remember the passage from Isaiah earlier in the book? Let's revisit chapter 55 in context:

> Come, all you who are thirsty, come to the waters; and you who have no money, come, buy and eat! Come, buy wine and milk without money and without cost. Why spend money on what is not bread, and your labor on what does not satisfy? Listen, listen to me, and eat what is good, and your soul will delight in the richest of fare. Give ear and come to me; hear me, that your soul may live. I will make an everlasting covenant with you, my faithful love promised to David. See, I have made him a witness to the peoples, a leader and commander of the peoples. Surely you will summon nations you know not, and nations that do not know you will hasten to you, because of the Lord your God, the Holy One of Israel, for he has endowed you with splendor.
>
> Seek the Lord while he may be found; call on him while he is near. Let the wicked forsake his way and the evil man his thoughts. Let him turn to the Lord, and he will have mercy on him, and to our God, for he will freely pardon.
>
> "For my thoughts are not your thoughts, neither are your ways my ways," declares the Lord. "As the heavens are higher

> than the earth, so are my ways higher than your ways and my thoughts than your thoughts. As the rain and the snow come down from heaven, and do not return to it without watering the earth and making it bud and flourish, so that it yields seed for the sower and bread for the eater, so is my word that goes out from my mouth: It will not return to me empty, but will accomplish what I desire and achieve the purpose for which I sent it. You will go out in joy and be led forth in peace; the mountains and hills will burst into song before you, and all the trees of the field will clap their hands. Instead of the thornbush will grow the pine tree, and instead of briers the myrtle will grow. This will be for the LORD's renown, for an everlasting sign, which will not be destroyed."

That passage is bursting with true life! Every time I read it, my heart literally aches with desire to experience more of what Isaiah describes. See, God truly does not care about our money. Your value and mine was forever established at the Cross. And the greatest rewards even in this life come as we learn to drink "living water" as Jesus taught the woman at the well in John 2. Rely completely on him.

The one essential to a successful escape from the Debt Trap is God. Take hold of his strong and mighty hands. Your confidence in him will be richly rewarded beyond money. You will achieve more than peace, freedom, and wellness in this life. The Lord will turn his face to yours and say, "Well done, good and faithful servant, come and share your Master's happiness."

ENDNOTE

1. *Half Time,* Nov./Dec. 2002, 46.

The Wealth Is in the Word

Deuteronomy 8:17–18 "You may say to yourself, 'My power and the strength of my hands have produced this wealth for me.' But remember the Lord your God, for it is he who gives you the ability to produce wealth, and so confirms his covenant, which he swore to your forefathers, as it is today."

Joshua 1:8 "Do not let this Book of the Law depart from your mouth; meditate on it day and night, so that you may be careful to do everything written in it. Then you will be prosperous and successful."

Psalm 1:1–3 "Blessed is the man who does not walk in the counsel of the wicked or stand in the way of sinners or sit in the seat of mockers. But his delight is in the law of the LORD, and on his law he meditates day and night. He is like a tree planted by streams of water, which yields its fruit in season and whose leaf does not wither. Whatever he does prospers."

Jeremiah 27:5 "With my great power and outstretched arm I made the earth and its people and the animals that are on it, and I give it to anyone I please."

Jeremiah 29:11 "For I know the plans I have for you," declares the LORD, "plans to prosper you and not to harm you, plans to give you hope and a future."

Jeremiah 32:17 "Ah, Sovereign LORD, you have made the heavens and the earth by your great power and outstretched arm. Nothing is too hard for you."

Matthew 6:33 "But seek first his kingdom and his righteousness, and all these things will be given to you as well."

Luke 16:10–13 "Whoever can be trusted with very little can also be trusted with much, and whoever is dishonest with very little will also be dishonest with much. So if you have not been trustworthy in handling worldly wealth, who will trust you with true riches? And if you have not been trustworthy with someone else's property, who will give you property of your own? No servant can serve two masters. Either he will hate the one and love the other, or he will be devoted to the one and despise the other. You cannot serve both God and Money."

Philippians 4:19 "And my God will meet all your needs according to his glorious riches in Christ Jesus."

1 Timothy 6:17 "Command those who are rich in this present world not to be arrogant nor to put their hope in wealth, which is so uncertain, but to put their hope in God, who richly provides us with everything for our enjoyment."

ABOUT THE AUTHOR

Dr. Kregg Hood, author, speaker, and educator, is president of Prime Source Providers. Dr. Hood has also served as a minister, a missionary, and a college instructor.

Hood earned his doctorate from Texas Tech University in instructional communication in 1987. He also holds master's degrees in missions and in religious communication and a bachelor of arts degree with undergraduate majors in Bible, biblical languages, and mathematics.

He and his wife, Karen, are parents of a daughter, Kalah, and a son, Kyle.

Other books by Dr. Hood include *Take God at His Word,* Books 1 and 2.

Dr. Hood is available to teach or speak for special events and may be contacted by phone, 1-800-364-5664, or by fax, 1-817-232-2030.

A "Quick Start" to Escape the Debt Trap

If you find yourself struggling to make your payments, the first place to go is to a leader in your church's financial crisis ministry. They will encourage you, pray for you, and work to help you develop a way out of the Debt Trap.

However, if this is not a good option for you, please call Christian Debt Solutions, toll free, at 1-800-364-5664. Christian Debt Solutions is a nonprofit credit counseling organization dedicated to helping you with budget planning, credit counseling, and debt management. Our planning and counseling services are available at no charge. This service is especially helpful if you're falling behind on your credit card or house payments. The counselors will provide you with practical, Bible-centered insights and options to assist you during this stress-filled time in your life. Time is of the essence; please don't hesitate to call.